# Introducing LOGO

# Introducing LOGO

**Boris Allan**

**GRANADA**
London Toronto Sydney New York

Granada Technical Books
Granada Publishing Ltd
8 Grafton Street, London W1X 3LA

First published in Great Britain by
Granada Publishing 1984



*British Library Cataloguing in Publication Data*
Allan, Boris
Introducing LOGO.
1. LOGO (Computer program language)
I. Title
001.64'24 QA76.8.L63

ISBN 0-246-12323-0

Typeset by V & M Graphics Ltd, Aylesbury, Bucks
Printed and bound in Great Britain by
Mackays of Chatham, Kent

# Contents

I dedicate this book to my children,
Mark and Ruth, still being educated.

# Preface

This book is designed to help all those who wish to find out more about the language LOGO, a language which has been around and developing for almost twenty years.

LOGO is a language which has lately become rather more popular with a wide range of people. Though the established microcomputer languages (especially the many forms of BASIC) have long been available for a variety of applications, BASIC had often been used because there was no appropriately straightforward alternative. LOGO now provides that alternative.

More than any other language, LOGO is intended to demystify computers and computer programming, and make the power of computers accessible to all. A supporter of LOGO must be against the pointless use of jargon, and against any attempt to make computers 'special'. LOGO is an egalitarian language.

The range of applications for which LOGO is suited ranges from research into Artificial Intelligence, to the design of graphics applications, and to the teaching of pre-school children. LOGO has even been used in the teaching of the mentally handicapped, allowing the handicapped person control over that powerful device, a computer.

BASIC is often promoted as a language which is simple to learn, but LOGO is simpler to learn and is also of far greater power and applicability.

In the writing of this book I have been assisted by conversations with many people, too numerous to mention or for me to remember all their names.

I am grateful to many people whose names I do not know. I talked to teachers using primitive versions of LOGO in schools who found that education came alive for their pupils, even with that primitive version. They were enthusiasts for LOGO even though they may only have used a Turtle Graphics only version.

The members and officers of the British LOGO Users' Group (BLUG), were especially helpful (the address for BLUG is c/o Pam Valley, 26 Tithby Road, Bingham, Notts.). It was at a BLUG conference that I met the originator of LOGO, Seymour Papert, and was impressed by his sense of mission. I have also been helped by many manufacturers, and software providers who have, in some cases, provided me with preliminary information about their LOGO versions: Atari, Commodore, Computer Concepts, Digital Research, Research Machines, Roundhill Computer Systems, Sinclair Research, Tandy (UK), and Texas Instruments.

The turtle in LOGO is very important, and I would like to thank Jessop Microelectronics for the use of a photograph of their floor turtle (Figure 2.1).

LOGO implies a revolution in thinking and learning for all who are exposed to the language. I hope that this book explains the reasons behind the revolution, and why the revolution will succeed.

## Chapter One

# Introduction

I was testing a version of LOGO for the IBM Personal Computer (actually, Waterloo LOGO), and was being helped to set up the IBM PC with a colour monitor and colour card. After we had set up the system, I loaded Waterloo LOGO.

I cleared the screen, and on the screen there appeared a triangle shape or arrow-head. I typed in

```
FD 50
```

and the arrow-head moved up the screen leaving a line behind, from where it started to where it finished. FD stands for (is a shortened version of) FORWARD, and the arrow-head had moved forward 50 units.

There was already a fair amount of interest at this simple movement of the arrow-head, from those who had helped me set up the PC. These were people who were familiar with fairly sophisticated computers, and who possessed a fair degree of competence in general computing. A child who was in the shop (looking at rather more mundane machines) was not so impressed – 'We do that at school!'.

Next I typed in

```
RT 90
```

and the arrow-head turned through 90 degrees, so that the point faced to the right. The experts were engrossed at that simple change. Then I typed

```
FD 50
```

and another line was drawn in the direction of the arrow-head, the same length as the previous line. Excitement grew. We agreed that to draw a square we needed to repeat those moves, and so, after

```
RT 90
```

one of the others entered

```
FD 50 RT 90 FD 50 RT 90
```

all at once.

We had drawn a square, and had left the arrow-head pointing straight upwards – in the same direction as it faced at the start of the drawing.

The experts then tried out other things. For example, they tried to draw a triangle: they failed at the first attempt, but soon succeeded and became quite animated. The experts had seen many other programs and languages, but their experience did not stop them appreciating the intrinsic interest of the language they were using – *LOGO.*

Many children in schools will soon be using LOGO, and they find LOGO just as interesting as the experts. Children manage to learn a great deal about mathematics and thinking from LOGO, and the appeal of LOGO is indeed very great.

The arrow-head is not an arrow-head, but is a visual representation of a *turtle*, a turtle which you direct across the display screen by use of simple commands. The turtle on the screen can also have a physical counterpart on the floor, a *floor turtle*, and that turtle draws real lines on real paper. *Turtle graphics* is an excellent way of teaching children to appreciate the beauty of mathematics. LOGO is very successful with children.

My experts were beginning to learn the limitations of instant ('here and now') commands. Instead of drawing a square by putting in eight commands (four FDs and four RTs), they wanted to say:

```
SQUARE
```

to draw a square. I therefore went on to show them how to form new commands in LOGO, using a square as an example. I entered, first,

```
TO SQUARE
```

I entered this because I needed to tell the system how TO do a thing called SQUARE. Then I went on to complete the instructions:

```
TO SQUARE
  REPEAT 4[FD 50 RT 90]
END
```

Being experts they could appreciate without explanation that the LOGO words meant REPEAT 4 times the commands between [and]. A child has no problems either.

I then entered

SQUARE RT 180 SQUARE

and a SQUARE was drawn, the turtle/arrow-head turned through 180 degrees (i.e. to face in the opposite direction) and another SQUARE was drawn. We had drawn two squares, in different places, just by use of one command and a turn. They were enthralled!

We decided to change the procedure SQUARE so that it drew squares of various sizes, just as with FD 40 the 40 indicates how far to move. At this point, I explained about parameters and how to use the facility to EDIT the procedure (actually I had to read the manual to EDIT, because editing systems vary so much).

I left them playing, and came back later. They were by then drawing circles, five-pointed stars and many other shapes, and were using shapes within shapes. They wanted to know if there was anything other than turtle graphics to LOGO: for example, could they use trigonometrical functions (as in BASIC), so I said yes. By then they were firmly convinced that no BASIC was able (as a matter of course) to produce graphics of the quality of those produced by LOGO, without a lot of extra work being put into the BASIC programming.

'Were there any other facilities in LOGO?' Well, there was list processing, I answered, at which one person's ears pricked up. He was trying to learn LISP (on the BBC Microcomputer) because it was a list processing language. Could he do in LOGO what he could do in LISP? The answer was: Yes, if it is a full version of LOGO. He became very excited. List processing is thought to be an esoteric topic, though it does have many useful applications. Here, he had been presented with an excellent graphics language – LOGO – which has list processing too!

Here is a language which can be used in research into artificial intelligence; can perform all the numerical functions of BASIC and just as easily; has excellent graphics; and yet is so simple that young children can use it. Can any other language make that claim?

# Chapter Two
# An Outline to LOGO

> A weightless and perfectly flexible rope is hung over a weightless, frictionless pulley attached to the roof of a building. At one end of the rope is a weight which exactly counterbalances a monkey at the other end. If the monkey begins to climb, what will happen to the weight?
>
> *The Magic of Lewis Carroll*, edited by John Fisher

How do you think? How do you think you think? How do you learn? Do you have problems with learning? What is 'learning'?

What do you think happens to the weight?

Seymour Papert (in *Mindstorms*, 1980, page 131) tells us that he has presented Lewis Carroll's puzzle to several hundred undergraduates at MIT (the Massachusetts Institute of Technology). All of these undergraduates had successfully passed exacting introductory physics courses.

Three quarters of those who had not seen the problem before gave incorrect answers, or could not decide how to tackle the problem. The problem is definitely 'hard', and was one of Lewis Carroll's two favourite problems (the other being 'Where does the day begin?').

The problem is not, however, in any way 'complex'. The reasons why so many were (and will be) wrong is that the *solver* makes the problem complex. Many people do not see the easy (and correct) answer because it is so easy. Sometimes the easy answer is discarded because it is so simple, and answers have to be complicated.

## Thinking and schemas

Seymour Papert is the driving force behind the language LOGO, and his interest in the Monkey Puzzle is due to his interest in thinking. LOGO is a computer language which is designed to allow the user to program the computer, rather than allowing the computer to program the user.

In the LOGO vision, the child (and the main emphasis is on the child learning) gets the computer to do things that the child wants to do. In conventional computer-assisted learning (CAL), the computer (i.e. the program) makes the child do what the computer seems to want to do.

LOGO tries to help children (and older users) to discover tools of thought which are applicable beyond the mere programming of a computer. One of the key tools of thought which LOGO encourages is the notion that we can learn just as much from our errors as from our successes: for to err is human and should not automatically incur sanctions.

How many of you will feel slightly guilty if I tell you that the answer to Carroll's problem is that monkey and rock both rise – at exactly the same speed? Remember, most of Papert's students were wrong as well (note, I assume you were wrong). Try to think how you attempted to solve the problem. Try to work out if you fear failure.

Students at MIT tended to think of the problem in terms of 'conservation of energy', or 'conservation of moments', and so on. Only a few saw it as a 'law of motion' problem, because most were not accustomed to think in those terms – it was not included in their tools of thought.

When it is pointed out that the monkey and the rock are intimately related, because they are linked by the rope, the answer becomes rather clearer. Young children, without the benefit of a physics education, often give the correct answer because they see it as the monkey pulling the rock towards itself. The distance between the rock and monkey gets smaller, and (as they are balanced) they go up together. As the monkey climbs the rope (jerks, tugs, or whatever), the monkey and weight remain directly opposite each other.

There are two key principles in learning:

1. Ideas which are more difficult than those a person already knows, cannot be learnt from a definition – these higher order concepts can only be learnt from suitable examples.

2. In any discipline, suitable examples almost always involve other, less complex, ideas, so it has to be ensured that the simpler ideas are already known by the learner.

The first principle is broken by the vast majority of text books and programming manuals. Topics are introduced, not by examples, but by definitions – usually unintelligible to the learner. Some people may cope, but many do not.

Producing a suitable collection of examples requires both inventiveness and a very clear awareness of the ideas to be communicated. It also helps if the examples start simply, though to start simply does not mean that the end will not be complex. In learning we build up mental 'structures' which relate ideas and concepts, and in psychology the term for a mental structure is a *schema*. (See, for example, *The Psychology of Learning Mathematics* by Richard R. Skemp.)

Schemas are essential tools for the acquisition of further knowledge. Everything we learn depends on knowing something else already. The question is where to start in the learning of 'learning'. In a sense, to 'understand' a topic is to put that topic within some known schema – but sometimes the schema is wrong, of course.

LOGO tries to develop schemas, with particular emphasis on mathematics, by allowing the user to explore the world of the turtle, learning by examples constructed by the user – and learning from his mistakes.

## The turtle

Everybody has to start somewhere, and with LOGO one starts with the *turtle*.

Papert (*Mindstorms*, page 6) thinks it is possible to design computers so that learning to communicate with them can be a natural process, '... more like learning French by living in France than like trying to learn it through the unnatural process of foreign-language instruction in classrooms'. Papert also thinks that learning to communicate with a computer may change the way other learning takes place.

Children, he says, are learning – through LOGO – to love communicating with computers, and when this communication occurs, children learn mathematics as a living language. Mathematics is the key to the future (computers are mathematics embodied) and children are far more able mathematicians than many imagine. The reason why so many do so badly is the way the subject is *not* taught.

As Papert (*Mindstorms*, page 7) notes: 'If we had to base our opinions on observation of how poorly children learned French in American schools, we would have to conclude that most people were incapable of mastering it. But we know that all normal children would learn it very easily if they lived in France.'

So, we start with the turtle. The turtle is a computer-controlled (and therefore child-controlled) cybernetic animal which lives on the VDU or television screen. The turtle serves no purpose other than that of being easy to program, and being something with which it is easy to relate (and think). Some turtles have an even more substantial existence, as computer-controlled physical objects – a simple mobile robot, as shown in Figure 2.1.

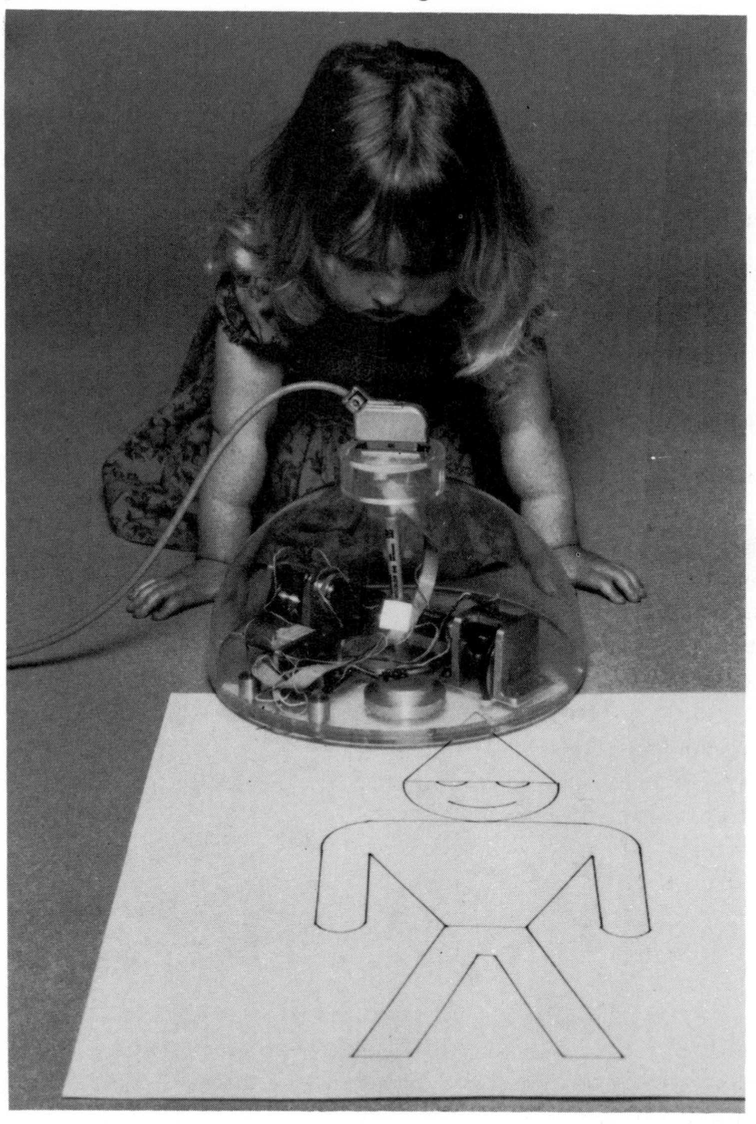

*Fig. 2.1.* A floor turtle (photograph of the Edinburgh Turtle, manufactured by Jessop Microelectronics, London).

The turtle conforms to the second of the learning principles: you cannot get a much simpler idea than that of the turtle, and in the case of the robot you can touch it as well as see it.

You instruct the turtle (by typing in on the computer) to go FORWARD 100 – or FD 100 – and the turtle goes forward 100 units on the floor, or on the screen (or both). You tell the turtle to RIGHT 90 – or RT 90 – and the turtle turns through 90 degrees to the right. The number may not mean much to a child early on, but the child soon learns.

The turtle has moved forward 100, and then turned right through 90 degrees. If the child then repeats the instructions, the turtle has described an 'L' shape. Two more repetitions, and a square has been drawn (see Figure 2.2). The child can invent new commands to draw new shapes (where, for instance, FORWARD is an already existing command).

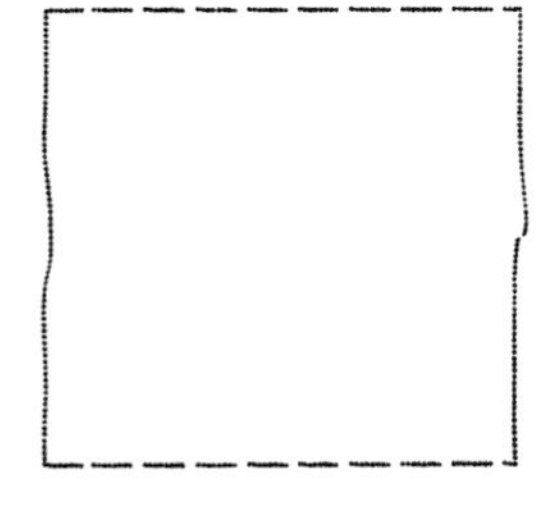

*Fig. 2.2.* A square.

Suppose a new command is to be defined to draw a square. All that is needed is four FORWARD 100 then RIGHT 90 sets of commands. On the Tandy Color Computer, there is a cartridge available for a version of LOGO – the TRS-80 Color LOGO. This cartridge also seems to work on the Dragon 32. In the Tandy version of LOGO we would enter

```
TO SQUARE
  FORWARD 100 RIGHT 90
  FORWARD 100 RIGHT 90
  FORWARD 100 RIGHT 90
  FORWARD 100 RIGHT 90
  END
```

This set of commands would also work on most other versions of LOGO.

To draw a square, therefore, having defined the command, all one needs to do now is enter SQUARE, and we draw a square of side 100. If we now enter

RIGHT 45 SQUARE

the square of side 100 is turned through 45 degrees to the right (see Figure 2.3). To enter another

RIGHT 45 SQUARE

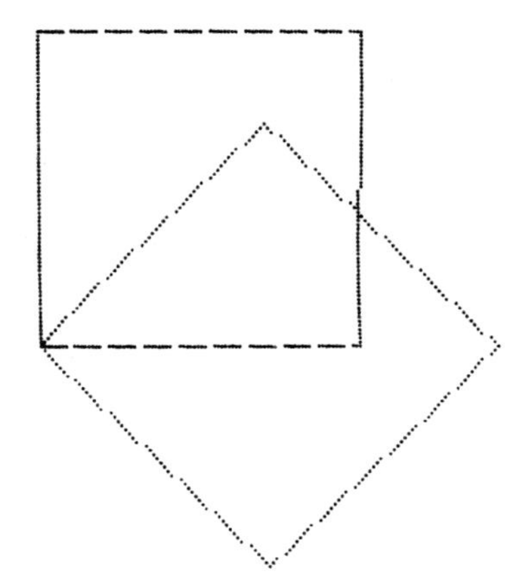

*Fig. 2.3.* Two squares.

is to draw a square turned through a further 45 degrees (i.e. a total of $45 + 45 = 90$ degrees from the original square – see Figure 2.4).

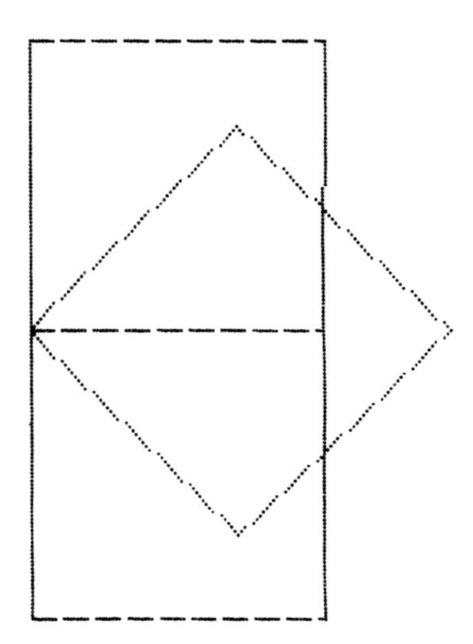

*Fig. 2.4.* Three squares.

## Proceeding to think

Already we have progressed from the simple ideas of a move and a turn to the more complex idea that a square is an assembly of moves and turns. The slightly more complex command SQUARE is a 'procedure' and a procedure is one way of taking something more complex, and making it appear a whole.

To draw a square, therefore, we realise that it is built up of several very simple elements: four lines, each with a turn at the end. To concentrate on procedures accentuates the structure of the problem, which assists greatly in the learning process, and in thinking generally.

Part of the structure of the square is that all the sides are effectively the same, i.e. they are all of the same length, with the same turn at the end. In Tandy Color LOGO (TCL):

```
TO SQUARE
  REPEAT 4 (FORWARD 100 RIGHT 90)
END
```

will draw a square for obvious reasons. This command/procedure definition will not work on many other LOGOs, for a very simple reason. Most LOGOs use square brackets [  ] where TCL uses the round brackets (  ).

In another version of LOGO (i.e. LOGO 2, by Computer Concepts for the BBC Microcomputer), to draw a square we would write:

```
TO SQUARE
  REPEAT 4, FORWARD 100: RIGHT 90
END
```

where there are no brackets of any form, just a comma ','.

LOGO 2 has a different way of looking at the REPEAT instruction. In LOGO 2 anything which follows the comma is repeated the specified number of times – as long as it is separated from the preceding command by a colon ':'. Most other versions of LOGO (and there is no standard LOGO) separate out the portion to be repeated by some form of brackets (usually square).

Another way of producing a square, in Research Machines LOGO (for the RML 380Z and 480Z microcomputers), is

```
BUILD SQUARE
  REPEAT 4 FORWARD 100 AND RIGHT 90
END
```

and instead of the word TO there is the word BUILD. In RML LOGO you *build* a square, rather than explaining how *to* make a square. Also, the portion after the REPEAT 4 is very like that of LOGO 2, but instead of the colon there is the 'AND'. RML LOGO is very different from most other versions, though it is a complete version.

In TI LOGO (for the Texas Instruments TI 99/4A), a rather more 'standard' implementation, the definition would be:

```
TO SQUARE
  REPEAT 4 [FORWARD 100 RIGHT 90]
END
```

and is the most common form of the definition, which should work for most LOGOs.

### Variable thinking

Whatever we say about the procedure/command SQUARE, it is certainly rather inflexible. How many of us are satisfied with just one size of a square, even though we can tilt it and move it around?

To draw squares of different size sides in TCL, we modify the definition of SQUARE to:

```
TO SQUARE2 :SIDE
  REPEAT 4 (FD :SIDE RT 90)
END
```

and we have introduced a new idea, the idea of a variable (which in this case is called :SIDE). The variable has a preceding colon ':' to indicate that it is a variable rather than a command – :SIDE is not a directive to do anything.

The command FORWARD (or, in the shortened version, FD) is usually followed by a number, where the number can vary and indicates how far forward we intend to go. The command is said to take one 'parameter', one item which sets limits on what is to be done. The command RIGHT (or RT) also has one parameter, which gives the extent to which the turn is to the right.

In SQUARE2 there is one parameter, the variable :SIDE, and :SIDE represents all the possible values we might wish for the sides of the square. We call it :SIDE to make the meaning easier to follow. We could have called it :XYZ and it would still have worked. For example,

```
TO ABC :XYZ
  REPEAT 4 (FD   :XYZ RT 90)
END
```

would also draw a square of varying side, but its function takes some working out.

How do we use SQUARE2? We simply

```
SQUARE2 150
```

to draw a square of side 15∅. If we enter

```
SQUARE2 100 SQUARE2 200
```

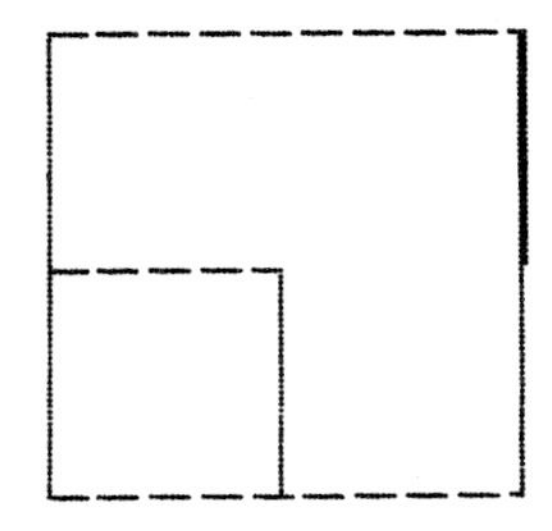

*Fig. 2.5.* A square in a square.

we produce two squares with the same corner, one twice as big as the other (see Figure 2.5). When we introduce a left turn of 45 degrees into the arrangement

```
SQUARE2 100 LEFT 45 SQUARE2 200
```

we produce Figure 2.6.

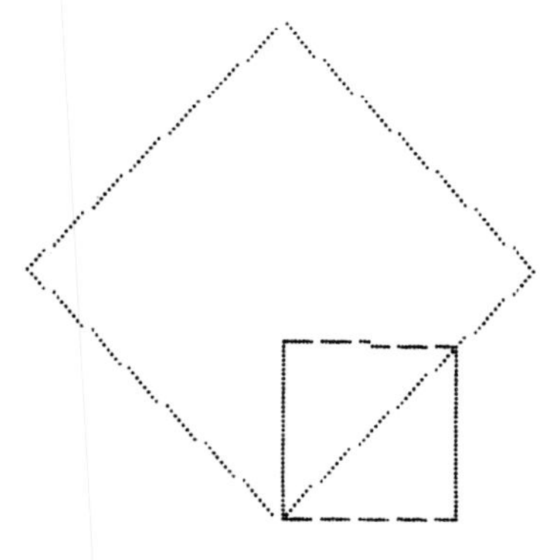

*Fig. 2.6.* Rotated square.

## More variability

There is no reason why we need to only have one parameter (and therefore one variable). Consider the command MANYSIDES.

```
TO MANYSIDES   :SIDE   :TURN
  WHILE KEY = 0 (FD   :SIDE RT   :TURN)
END
```

This has two parameters (the variables :SIDE and :TURN), a new controlling command (WHILE), and a special TCL function (KEY).

If no key on the keyboard has been depressed, then the special TCL function KEY is equal to zero (i.e. it is true that KEY = 0). WHILE it is true that KEY = 0, the portion in round brackets is repeated. To stop the procedure MANYSIDES a key has to be pressed.

WHILE is a useful command which is not common to all LOGOs, though it is always possible to define such a procedure using lists (of which, later). WHILE is also a command in RML LOGO.

To draw a square of side 100, therefore, we can use

```
MANYSIDES 100 90
```

and when the square is complete, we press a key to stop. To draw an equilateral triangle (i.e. one whose angles are all 60 degrees) let's use

```
MANYSIDES 100 60
```

Instead of an equilateral triangle, however, we have produced the shape shown in Figure 2.7. This shape is not an equilateral triangle,

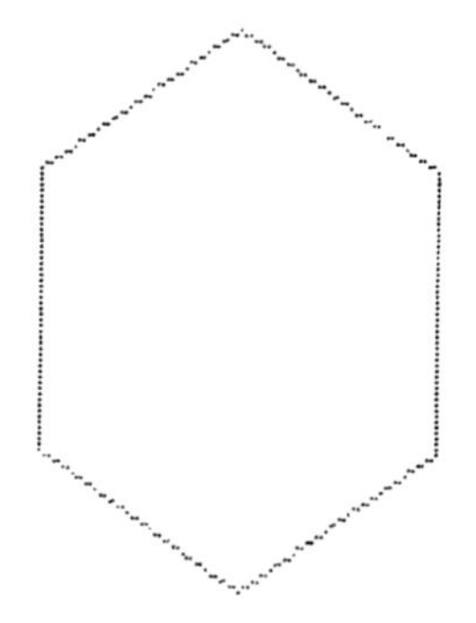

*Fig. 2.7.* MANYSIDES :TURN 60.

rather it is a hexagon. This is a common error – I remember making it myself. We can learn from this error, as follows.

The turn we make is the 'exterior' angle of the shape, not the 'interior' angle, so the correct instructions are:

MANYSIDES 100 120

and we produce Figure 2.8. Trying

MANYSIDES 200 112

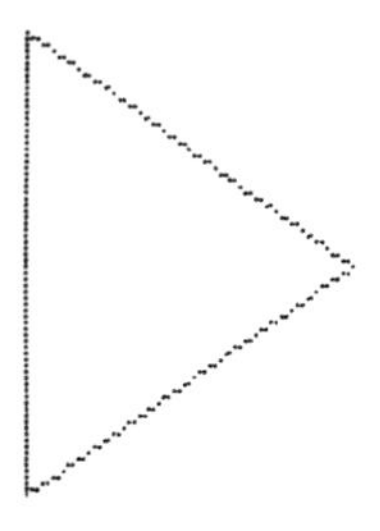

*Fig. 2.8.* MANYSIDES :TURN 120.

produces the rather more complex shape in Figure 2.9.

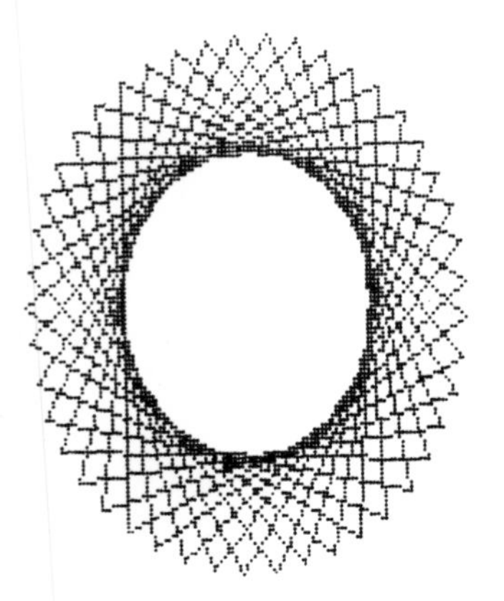

*Fig. 2.9.* MANYSIDES :TURN 112.

## Editorial functions

To talk glibly of entering new commands, or altering old commands to produce slightly different results, ignores a basic problem with all computer languages. Changes do not 'just happen', they have to be made.

Procedures do not appear out of thin air, they have to be entered into the computer's memory, and stored somewhere. The reason I have used TCL as an example so far (and remember it works on the Dragon 32 as well) is because the distinction between the various elements in using LOGO is made very clear.

When LOGO starts on the Tandy Color Computer the user is left in BREAK mode. On the screen there is

LOGO:

and it is not possible to run any LOGO procedures. BREAK mode is effectively the organising mode: it is used to control devices such as the printer or cassette recorder, and is the means by which the other modes are entered. To press the BREAK key at any time sends you back to this mode.

The next mode is the RUN mode, the mode in which you type in the commands, actually to get the turtle to perform some action or other. Some commands (such as WHILE) cannot be used directly in RUN mode; such commands can only be used within the body of a procedure. In RUN mode it is only possible to have one command on a line.

The lines

```
FD 200
SQUARE2 300
```

are both admissible in RUN mode, but the line

```
TO RECTANGLE  :LENGTH  :BREADTH
```

is illegal. The above line is part of a procedure definition, and one can only form procedure definitions in another mode (EDIT). Leaving RUN mode to return to BREAK mode, one enters EDIT mode from the BREAK mode.

In EDIT mode the definitions are not checked for accuracy, but definition checking happens in RUN mode.

A final mode, and one that can be entered directly from RUN mode, is DOODLE mode. By use of the keys on the top line, the turtle can be instructed to move according to the directions given on the keys. This is exclusive to TCL (as far as I know), and allows small children control over the turtle even when they cannot spell.

All LOGOs have to have some form of edit mode, but often it is possible to enter procedure definitions in the equivalent of a RUN mode. To edit a definition called BOOBY, for example,

```
EDIT  "BOOBY
```

is entered. The double quote " informs the system to look at the procedure of that name, and not to activate that procedure – though for some LOGOS the quotes are not needed. Other names might be used, e.g. RML uses CHANGE and also has RESTORE which means 'forget that last CHANGE'.

## Making a list

Some LOGOs, e.g. TCL and LOGO 2, are principally mechanisms for turtle graphics, and – at an introductory level – they have a good deal to offer.

Once the user wishes to progress beyond mere pictures, LOGO offers far more than just a nice way to use procedures. LOGO offers list processing, with many functions taken from an Artificial Intelligence (AI) language called LISP.

A list in LOGO is normally that between square brackets, which might explain why both TCL and LOGO 2 have unconventional methods of showing the list of instructions after a REPEAT (i.e. they do not possess list processing). In the line

```
REPEAT 1 [FD 100  LT 37 BK 100]
```

or

```
REPEAT 1 [FORWARD 100  LEFT 37 BACK 100]
```

the command REPEAT expects a list following the first parameter (in this case 1). The list is the second parameter.

There is a special LOGO word, normally called something such as RUN, which takes a LOGO list as a parameter, and then treats the list as if it were a sequence of commands typed in at the keyboard. The sequence

```
RUN [FD 100  LT 37 BK 100]
```

is exactly the same as the REPEAT 1 sequence. RML LOGO is, again, rather different as it expects the 'name' of a sequence, not the sequence itself. This may be due to RML LOGO not using a list to follow REPEAT (because REPEAT 1 is the same as RUN).

A simple example of how RUN might be used in a more common form of LOGO is

```
TO VARYING.ACTION   :INSTRUCTIONS
  RUN   :INSTRUCTIONS
END
```

so that

```
VARYING.ACTION[REPEAT 4[FD 100 RT 90]]
```

will draw a square, whereas

```
VARYING.ACTION[FD 200]
```

will draw only a line. This is a powerful little facility, with great potential in more complex procedures.

A proper LOGO has list-processing, but turtle graphics in themselves are so immediate and useful that a good version of LOGO-style turtle graphics can be a useful teaching and learning device. List-processing is so wasteful of computer memory that in many cheaper (and smaller) LOGOS it is only worthwhile implementing a version of turtle graphics.

As we will discover, however, a LOGO-style turtle graphics requires more than a few turtle commands: it requires the implementation of the LOGO philosophy.

## Chapter Three

# LOGO Here and Now

> It is best to do things systematically, since we are only human, and disorder is our worst enemy.
>
> *Works and Days* by Hesiod

There are languages and languages. Some languages, like LOGO, work as soon as you type something into the machine. Some languages, like BASIC, work when you 'run' a program. For some languages, such as Pascal, the program instructions have to be stored away, then 'compiled', and only then run. The last method is the most tedious to use, and the first is the most immediate. LOGO is a *here and now* language – which, for the user, is the least difficult method of entering programs.

### Getting the sequence right

When a line

```
FORWARD 100
```

is entered, the line is drawn as soon as the carriage return is pressed (all lines are ended by a carriage return, or the computer would not know when the end of a line had been reached). Nothing happens when we enter

```
RIGHT 90
```

except that we might see the 'turtle' change the direction in which it is pointing. It all happens there and then, here and now.

It is possible to draw quite complicated shapes at the keyboard, or 'doodle' as it is called in Tandy Color LOGO. Though this might seem rather childish, or pointless, something is being learned. That which is being learned is the idea of *sequential thinking*. If it is necessary to perform action B before action C, and to perform action B one needs to have performed action A, then obviously the sequence of actions is A, B, C. This sounds very simple, yet such a sequence can often be lost in confusion. Consider the three commands:

```
FORWARD 100
RIGHT 90
FORWARD 150
```

These produce the result shown in Figure 3.1(a). Now make a small change in the order:

```
FORWARD 100
FORWARD 150
RIGHT 90
```

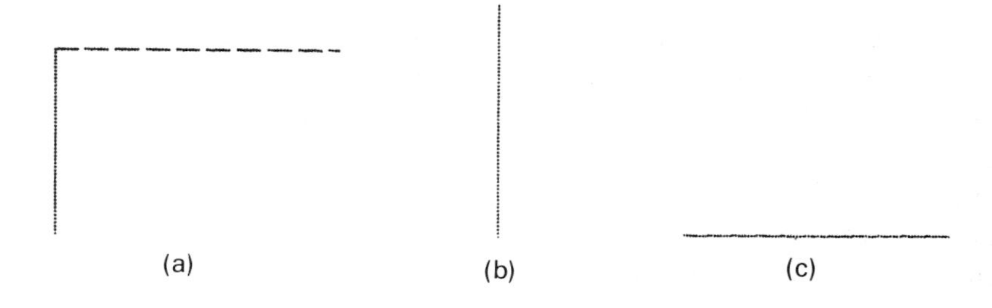


*Fig. 3.1.* Three commands.

The result is rather changed (Figure 3.1(b)) – a straight line is drawn rather than an L-shape. The line points directly upwards, because this is the way we will suppose that the turtle starts: in the middle pointing upwards (common to many LOGOs).

As a final change, examine:

```
RIGHT 90
FORWARD 100
FORWARD 150
```

and try to predict the result before checking with Figure 3.1(c). How many different ways are there to arrange these three commands?

*Answers:* A straight line going from left to right, and six arrangements of these three commands. Some arrangements have identical results, because FORWARD 100 FORWARD 150 is identical to FORWARD 150 FORWARD 100 (and both are the same as FORWARD 250). When drawing a shape interactively, such mistakes in the ordering are soon spotted, and the fact that commands are in an incorrect order is soon discovered.

To be able to think logically partly involves the ability to 'think through' consequences. With children, one way of helping them to learn to think is to get them to trace out the workings of the screen turtle on the floor. They can either use a mechanical turtle, or they themselves can be the turtle, tracing out the moves by walking forward so many steps, and turning through so many degrees. At one time this sequencing was shown by what are called 'flow charts', but LOGO dispenses with the need for flow charts because the sequencing is made plain within the language (see Chapter 4).

## An instant calculator

Just as it is possible to work one's way through a turtle shape instantly, it is possible to use LOGO as little more than an instant calculator. To enter, in – say – Apple LOGO:

```
PRINT 12−13/5
```

results in the output

```
>>9.4
```

because the computer acts sequentially (in this book, computer output is preceded by >>). 12 is taken, then 13 is taken and divided by 5. The result of the division (2.6) is then subtracted from 12. The order is important, as is shown in the following examples:

```
PRINT 13−12/5
```

```
>>10.6
```

but,

```
PRINT (13−12)/5
```

```
>>0.2
```

and to disentangle such simple arithmetic examples one needs to have a feeling for the order in which actions occur.

If we entered the following very simple sum, in any LOGO,

```
3+4
```

an error should be produced. The system will tell you that it does not know what to do with 7. It's sensible really; it has calculated the number 7 but then it is just left hanging around waiting to do something with the number. It could, for instance,

FORWARD (3+4)

or

LEFT (3+4)

but it needs to be *told* to do something. The system has nowhere to put the 7, thus the complaint, 'What's up, Doc?'.

Trying the commands

```
FORWARD 50 RIGHT  (0+10)
FORWARD 50 RIGHT  (10+10)
FORWARD 50 RIGHT  (20+10)
FORWARD 50 RIGHT  (30+10)
FORWARD 50 RIGHT  (40+10)
```

and onwards produces Figure 3.2. If the progression is continued, the result is Figure 3.3. There are easier ways to draw Figure 3.3, but more of that later.

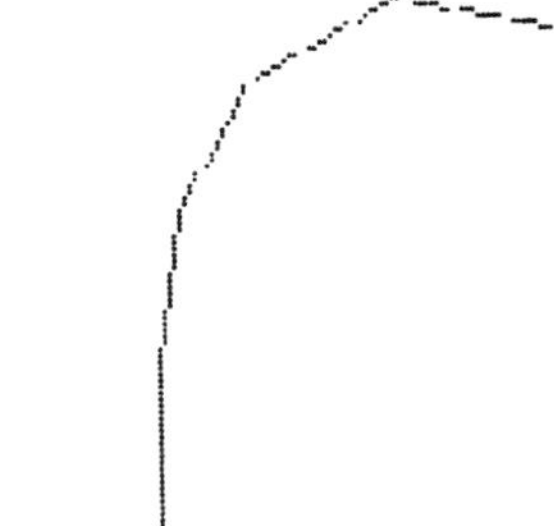

*Fig. 3.2.* A few lines and turns.

## A list of items

Returning to the last part of Chapter 2, the portion after the REPEAT and number was called a list, and a list was indicated by square brackets.

LOGO always expects to have to do something, the 'What's up Doc?' syndrome. So, to enter a list as, for example

[THIS IS A LIST]

produces an error. The system has to be told to do something with the list. The obvious thing to perform with a list is to print it out. For example:

```
PRINT [THIS IS A LIST]
>> THIS IS A LIST
```

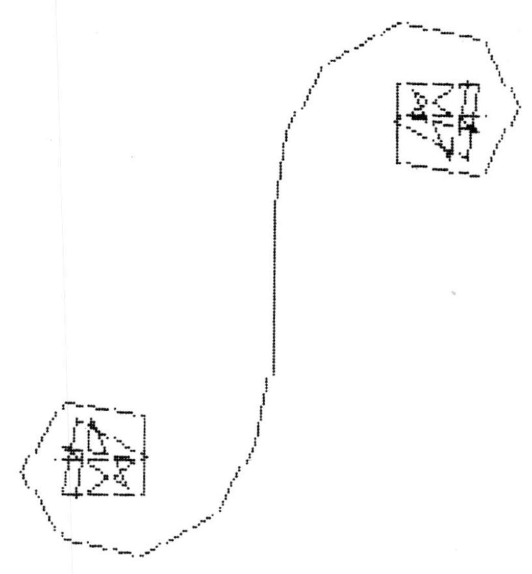

*Fig. 3.3.* Many straight lines.

and, if we entered

PRINT FIRST [THIS IS A LIST]

we would produce

>>THIS

The LOGO procedure FIRST takes the following list (i.e. [THIS IS A LIST]), and isolates the first element of the list. Entering

FIRST [THIS IS A LIST]

will again give an error, because we have not asked LOGO to do anything with THIS. The converse of the procedure FIRST is BUTFIRST (though it is called REST by RML),

PRINT BUTFIRST [THIS IS A LIST]
>> IS A LIST

and

PRINT FIRST BUTFIRST [THIS IS A LIST]
>> IS

However,

PRINT BUTFIRST FIRST [THIS IS A LIST]
>> HIS

The FIRST of the list is THIS (a word) and BUTFIRST either acts on a list to give all but the first element or – more important here – acts on a word to give all but the first character.

As with simple arithmetic and simple turtle graphics, the order in which we enter list operations is very important. The order in which operations are performed is backwards, in that the first procedure to be activated is the one on the right, closest to the list.

### Names, values, and actions

FIRST can act on a word

```
PRINT FIRST "WORDEXAMPLE
>>W
```

where the double quotes " before WORDEXAMPLE indicate that the word as such is meant, not its value or its action as a procedure. To clarify:

- SQUARE is treated by LOGO as a procedure.
- "SQUARE is treated by LOGO as the name of something. (In RML LOGO it is written 'SQUARE.)
- :SQUARE is treated by LOGO as the value of the thing named SQUARE, and in some LOGOs it can also be written THING "SQUARE. (In RML LOGO it is also written VALUE 'SQUARE).

There are certain distinctions which have to be made. A procedure, for example, has a name, and if LOGO comes across that name by itself

```
A.PROCEDURE
```

then it will try to activate A.PROCEDURE. If we wish to edit the procedure, we use the name of the procedure (and not its action). Thus,

```
EDIT "A.PROCEDURE
```

will put us into editing mode in some LOGOS, but in some LOGOs the quote is omitted. TCL has a different system, and RML has CHANGE.

To assign a value to a name, we use the procedure MAKE. To make the value of the variable A.NAME equal to 7, we use

```
MAKE "A.NAME 7
```

That is, use the procedure MAKE to operate on the item named A.NAME, and store the number 7 in that item. To get hold of the value stored in the item A.NAME, we use the colon (or THING or VALUE). Thus,

PRINT :A.NAME
>>7

or (in Apple LOGO and similar)

PRINT THING "A.NAME
>>7

or (in RML LOGO)

PRINT VALUE 'A.NAME
>> 7

but we can go much further. Figure 3.4 shows what is at work here. The name of an ITEM is given by "ITEM ('ITEM in RML), and the

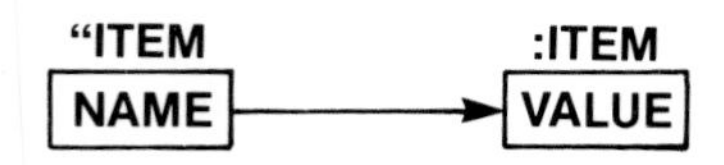


*Fig. 3.4.* Names and values.

item also stores a value, which is given by :ITEM. In a sense, the name 'points' to the value. The operation to move from the item to its value is the colon (or THING or VALUE).

Try to see if you can work out the reasons for the following sequences:

(1) MAKE "AUTHOR "BORIS.ALLAN
(2) PRINT :AUTHOR
(3) >>BORIS.ALLAN

and then:

(4) MAKE :AUTHOR [INTRODUCING LOGO]
(5) PRINT :AUTHOR
(6) >> BORIS.ALLAN
(7) PRINT :BORIS.ALLAN
(8) >> INTRODUCING LOGO

The item named AUTHOR stores the value "BORIS.ALLAN (1), and so when we print the value of AUTHOR (2) we print the name BORIS.ALLAN (3). The value stored in AUTHOR (i.e. the name

"BORIS.ALLAN) is made to store the value [INTRODUCING LOGO] (4). To print the value of AUTHOR (5) still gives the name BORIS.ALLAN (6). To print the value contained in BORIS.ALLAN (7) is to output [INTRODUCING LOGO] (8). Figure 3.5 shows the sequences at work in this example.

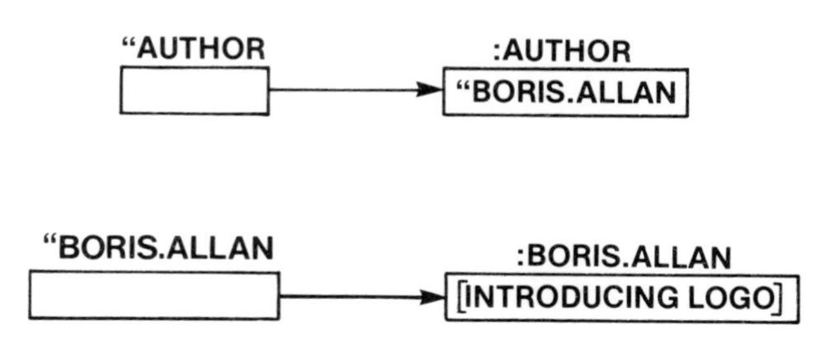


*Fig. 3.5.* Naming names.

These distinctions will become clearer as we progress, and now we progress to procedures.

## Translating LOGO

LOGO *is* 'here and now', BASIC *can* be 'here and now', and many other languages (e.g. Pascal or COBOL) are very much 'there and then'. The difference comes from the way in which each language is translated by the computer, translated from words we hope we understand, to machine instructions that the computer can understand. Put more simply, as there are many half-way houses, we can say that computer languages are either *interpreted*, or they are *compiled*.

The easiest to understand is the process of interpretation, which might be considered as the simplest way out of the translation problem. On the one hand, interpretation is the simplest method of translation and, on the other hand, quite often an interpreted language is easier to use – particularly for the novice.

Suppose we have typed in the line

```
FORWARD 100
```

to which we get an instant reaction: the turtle moves forward 100 units. The LOGO interpreter takes that line which has been typed in, and then the interpreter has to translate the LOGO instruction (instantly) into machine instructions (sometimes termed 'machine code'). There are many machine instructions needed to perform even the simplest LOGO command.

Once the line has been interpreted and obeyed, that line is forgotten. If, later, another line

FORWARD 100

is encountered, then that line is interpreted anew: therefore an interpreted language such as LOGO (or BASIC) tends to be slower than a language (such as FORTRAN) which is compiled.

The difference between an interpreter and a compiler can perhaps be understood in the context of another form of translation. If one were filling in a form, written in a foreign language, and one were being assisted to fill in the form, then the assistance might take one of two extremes. If the form were complex, but not all parts needed to be filled in, then the translator might interpret each line as he came to it. (Note that many lines would not be translated, because they would not be necessary.) This form of translation is least difficult in terms of the preparation needed; the translator need only know the language, and not the form. A rather more thorough method would be to compile a complete translation of the form into English. Far more work would go into the initial process of translation but, once compiled, the English version would be much quicker to use.

The key is the statement 'Far more work would go into the initial process of translation'. For a novice experimenting with a language (whether the language be BASIC or LOGO or whatever), the greater speed of a compiled version is immaterial given the much greater time to produce results. With a conventional compiled language it is impossible to use 'throw away' lines such as

FORWARD 100

because it is too difficult to implement.

## Translating procedures

'The moving finger writes, and having writ, nor all thy piety nor wit can cast it back to cancel half a line'. This is the same as saying that once

FORWARD 100

has been entered it is lost: it cannot be recalled.

What happens, therefore, when we define a procedure? Consider

```
TO TRI
  FD 100 RT 120
  FD 100 RT 120
  FD 100 RT 120
END
```

in which there are three FD 100 (i.e. FORWARD 100) instructions. We have to remember these three commands, because we will need to use TRI on more than one occasion. Why does the turtle remain still while we enter these commands? (Actually, in some peripheral versions of 'pretend' LOGOs, the turtle does move.) How do I use the new procedure/command TRI? I use it in this type of way:

```
TRI MOVE 150 TRI
```

In this case, the fact that I have used TRI twice is forgotten by the system as soon as the two TRIs have been obeyed. However, the system does not forget that TRI does a certain pattern of moves and turns.

The difference between FORWARD when it is within the procedure definition (i.e. between the TO and the END), and when it is used normally, has its parallels in BASIC. In BASIC, to enter the line

```
PRINT "#"
```

is instantly to print a # on the screen. To enter the line

```
100 PRINT "#"
```

is to store the line as part of a BASIC program, and the line will only be activated when the program is RUN and that line is reached.

In LOGO, the FD and RT commands in the procedure TRI are stored away, under the title 'TRI', and are not activated until that procedure is used. When the procedure is used, the content of the routine is interpreted in the normal manner (with due allowance for parameters, local variables, and so on). To change the contents of TRI is thus simple; the stored sequence is altered merely by use of some procedure such as EDIT.

# Chapter Four
# LOGO Proceeds with Procedures

Creative activity could be described as a type of learning process where teacher and pupil are located in the same individual.

*Drinkers of Infinity* by Arthur Koestler

Though, as we have seen, it is possible to use LOGO as an instant calculator, drawing machine, or player with words, we cannot progress very far before tedium begins.

LOGO can be used instantly, but to perform anything really worthwhile we need to have a rather more powerful set of LOGO procedures than those which come with the language. We want to be able to draw squares instantly, or have procedures by which we can collect information in lists (and keep the lists), or we would like procedures which do rather more than just add, subtract, multiply, or divide.

## Thinking constructively

When we think of 'a square' we think of the square in its entirety. We do not really think of the four lines of equal length and the four right angles (unless we are excessively mathematically conscious). We see a square, which on reflection we can resolve into sides and angles. In a similar way we see a table, and later might decide that it has legs and a flat surface. We do not normally walk into the room and say 'Oh look, an object with legs and a flat surface'. Instead, we perceive the whole.

What happens, though, when we try to solve a problem? How often do we see the problem as a whole, and only then consider the constituent parts? In Lewis Carroll's monkey puzzle, how many perceive the parts before they see the whole? How many never see the whole?

How many books have you read which are no more than separate little sections (each possibly admirable in itself) with little coherence in the book as a whole? How many computer games have you played, in which the game seems to be no more than separate unconnected little sub-games?

Though it seems that we naturally perceive wholes before parts, when it comes to problem-solving or creating new items we often think of the parts before the whole – and the whole suffers. If we act and think without reflection, we perceive wholes: if we have to think about how to think, often we find the wholes become invisible.

LOGO tries to emphasize the power of thinking of the whole, and also the power of then thinking of the whole as being made of parts (smaller 'wholes'). The parts might then be resolved into even smaller parts, and so on. The key aspect to LOGO is that all the parts are seen to be interrelated – a whole is composed of integrated parts.

Here is a LOGO procedure to make a table:

```
TO MAKE.TABLE
  TAKE.FLAT.WOOD
  REPEAT 4 [DRILL.HOLE.IN.CORNER]
  REPEAT 4 [MAKE.LEG   INSERT.IN.HOLE]
  STAND.ON.LEGS
END

TO MAKE.LEG
  WHILE [NOT ROUND] [TURN.ON.LATHE]
END
```

and we could invent even more elaborate sub-procedures. To make a table we still have to make the legs, but we do not first make the legs and then see if we can find some way of assembling them. (I have taken certain liberties with the LOGO language in the above procedures.)

When one learns to play chess, it is easy to learn the moves. It is more difficult to learn tactics in chess (i.e. combining moves to produce an advantage), and it is most difficult of all to learn to play strategically. Strategy is the combining of tactics and moves to produce a winning, rather than a short-term, advantage. To play chess well, one needs to be able to see the board as a whole (the strategy) but also one needs to be able to appreciate the individual elements, the tactics and the moves.

To think powerfully, to think constructively, we need to learn how to take problems and resolve each problem into sub-problems so that each sub-problem is simpler to solve than the major problem. Each sub-problem might then be resolved into even smaller problems if necessary.

To concentrate on each individual element by itself, without any attempt to see the whole, is a common failing of children – and of comedians. There is something comical about the person who tries to stop a table wobbling by cutting off pieces from the three longer legs – particularly when the person gets it wrong and the table still wobbles. In a silent movie, the comedian then saws off more pieces, until the table has no legs left.

In real life, a person makes one more adjustment to a program – to rid the program of yet another error – and the program gets more and more complex. As it becomes more complex it gets even more inefficient, and soon the program's writer cannot understand the program that has been written.

Figure 3.3 was the result of a large number of single isolated LOGO procedures (FORWARDs and RIGHTs) and this is one way to draw that Figure. There is a better way – there must be a better way – but the way most people approach problems and programs is to use many single instructions effectively. What is the better way?

## A better spiral

The initial sequence of LOGO procedures (see Chapter 3) was

```
FORWARD 50 RIGHT  (0+10)
FORWARD 50 RIGHT  (10+10)
FORWARD 50 RIGHT  (20+10)
```

and so on. If we examine each line, it is of the form

```
FORWARD 50 RIGHT (:ANGLE+10)
```

where :ANGLE takes the values 0, 10, 20, 30, 40 ... Suppose, instead of 50, we just say :DISTANCE

```
FORWARD :DISTANCE RIGHT (:ANGLE+:INC)
```

and we replace 10 by :INC.

When we further examine the above line, we begin to analyse the true nature of the problem, 'What is :ANGLE?'. ANGLE has the previous value of ANGLE plus the value of INC, so we might write

```
MAKE "ANGLE (:ANGLE+:INC)
FORWARD :DISTANCE RIGHT (:ANGLE+:INC)
```

and we find another pattern, that of (:ANGLE+:INC). If we could use (:ANGLE+:INC) only once, instead of twice, then we have simplified a good deal.

Try defining a procedure, with parameters :DISTANCE, :ANGLE, and :INC, which we will call INSPIRAL.

```
TO INSPIRAL :DISTANCE :ANGLE :INC
  FORWARD :DISTANCE
  RIGHT :ANGLE
  INSPIRAL :DISTANCE (:ANGLE+:INC) :INC
END
```

and let us see how this procedure works. Let us see what happens when we enter:

```
INSPIRAL 50 0 10
```

First the parameters DISTANCE, ANGLE, and INC take on the values 50, 0, and 10. The command FORWARD :DISTANCE moves 50 forward, the command RIGHT :ANGLE turns right through 0 degrees, and then INSPIRAL :DISTANCE (:ANGLE+: INC) :INC calls the procedure INSPIRAL with parameters 50, 10 (=0+10), and 10.

Procedure INSPIRAL is thus activated again, with different parameter values. The main difference is that in the later call :ANGLE is equal to the previous value of ANGLE plus the same INC. This may seem complex at first, so we will try again. Instead of writing

```
MAKE "ANGLE (:ANGLE+:INC)
```

we make the passing of parameters from procedure to procedure do this operation. Each time we activate the procedure, it is termed a 'call'. As part of the operation of the procedure 'call', it calls itself again. So, when we make the first call of INSPIRAL at the end of the procedure there is yet another call to INSPIRAL. When this new call of the procedure is almost completed, it again calls INSPIRAL. This succession of calls continues until the computer runs out of memory. If we number the first call as Call 1, the next call will be Call 2 and so on. Examine the values of the parameters at each call:

```
CALL 1   INSPIRAL 50 0 10
CALL 2   INSPIRAL 50 10 10
```

CALL 3 INSPIRAL 5Ø 2Ø 1Ø
CALL 4 INSPIRAL 5Ø 3Ø 1Ø
CALL 5 INSPIRAL 5Ø 4Ø 1Ø
CALL 6 INSPIRAL 5Ø 5Ø 1Ø

Note the similarity to the progression of FORWARDs and RIGHTs, above. To get a procedure to 'call itself' can thus be very helpful. In this case we can omit all the MAKEs, and the procedure is very short and sweet.

To get a procedure to call itself is so helpful and so valuable that it deserves a special name. The name is *recursion*, and Seymour Papert thinks that recursion is one of the most valuable aspects of LOGO or of computing languages in general. Thinking often seems to be recursive, and ideas often reflect on themselves. Recursion is not mysterious, it is really no more than an easy way to be repetitive – well, perhaps slightly more.

INSPIRAL is a very simple little procedure, but a procedure which can produce many outstandingly pretty and different results, depending on the values we choose for the angle and increment. Figures 4.1 to 4.5 show different curves for different values of these parameters.

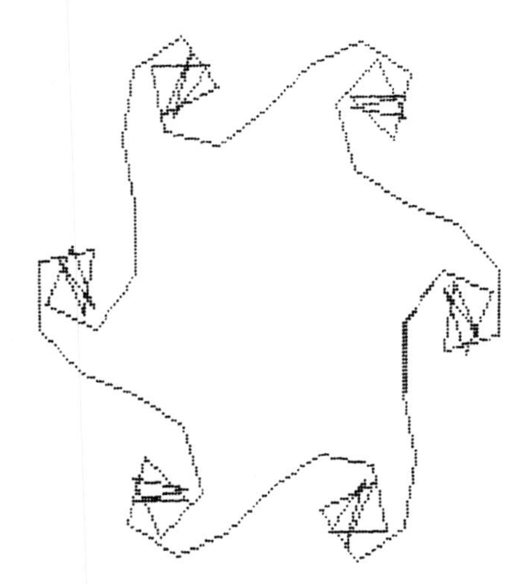

*Fig. 4.1.* INSPIRAL. :ANGLE=40 :INC=30.

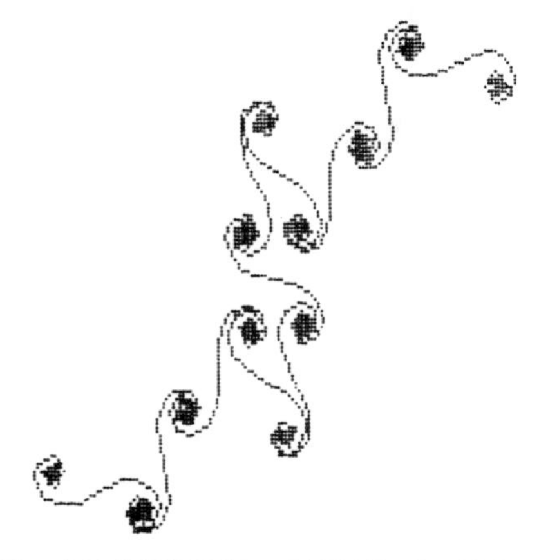

*Fig. 4.2.* INSPIRAL. :ANGLE=2 :INC=11.

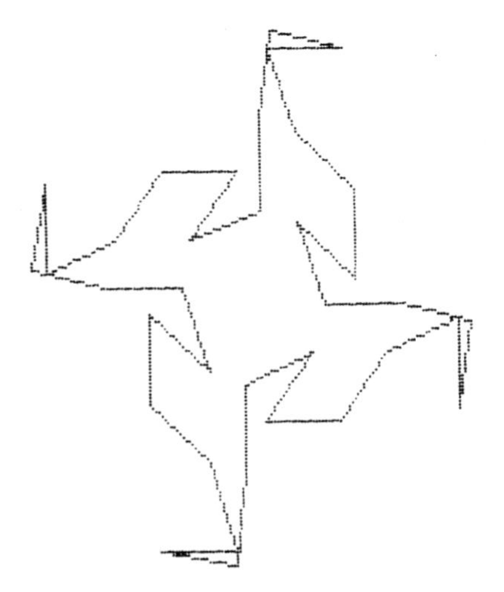

*Fig. 4.3.* INSPIRAL. :ANGLE=10 :INC=80.

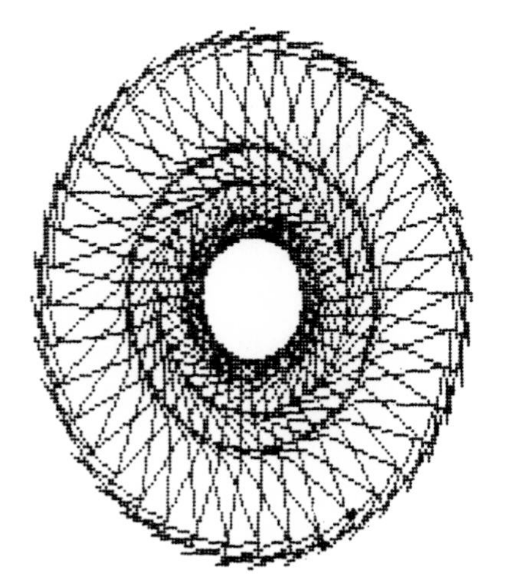

*Fig. 4.4.* INSPIRAL. :ANGLE=11 :INC=80.

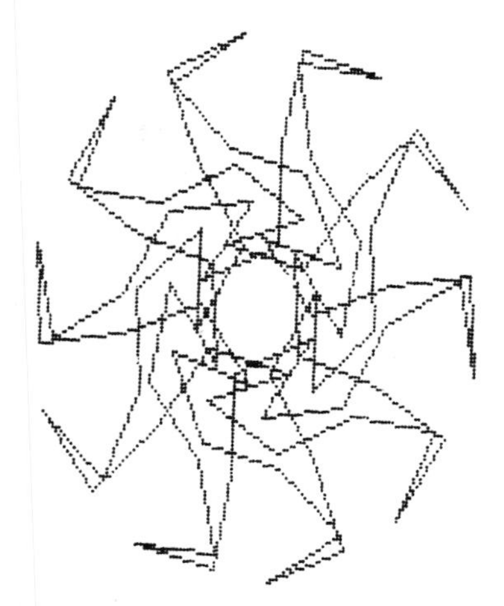

*Fig. 4.5.* INSPIRAL. :ANGLE=12 :INC=80.

## Learning with procedures

Imagine a child who has been shown the INSPIRAL procedure, and who is trying different values to see the different results. The child is the pupil, but the child is also the teacher because it is the child who is deciding and directing what is to be done.

Papert sees the use of LOGO in schools as a subversive activity, children taking control of their own computing environment, children creating what he calls their own 'microworlds'. What will a child learn from INSPIRAL, what will anybody learn?

The first, and most obvious, thing to be learnt is the value of conceptualisation. Any child, any person, who can draw pictures like those we have seen in Figures 4.1 to 4.5 with so little effort, will appreciate the value of the general approach. To draw these figures step by step – as we tried in Chapter 3 – would be immensely tedious, yet by forethought and some abstraction we have a general and powerful tool called INSPIRAL.

Any person can appreciate that point – even at an early age – so, when this person tries to draw other pictures, the incentive to abstract and conceptualise is there. Conceptualisation works. The child does not have to be told that this is 'abstraction' or 'conceptualisation'; the child teaches himself that there is a powerful way of approaching problems. The name is immaterial. It is the *idea* that counts.

A second thing to be learnt is rather more mundane. We learn some geometry, the geometry of 'inward spirals' (the reason for the name INSPIRAL). An inward spiral moves forward and keeps on turning (as do all spirals) but the angle through which the spiral bends gets greater and greater. Depending on the angles and rate of increasing bend (i.e. :INC) sooner or later the spiral turns back on itself.

Ultimately an inward spiral produces a closed curve; that is, the turtle starts repeating its movements. Abelson and diSessa, in *Turtle Geometry* (1980) show how even such a simply produced set of curves is a rich source of mathematical ideas. The curves are themselves so intriguing that their mathematical richness is almost a bonus, and the full richness cannot be properly appreciated by children at the primary level.

An 'outward spiral', as the name suggests, spirals outwards. A procedure to produce an outward spiral is

```
TO OUTSPIRAL :SIDE :INC :ANGLE
  FORWARD :SIDE
  RIGHT :ANGLE
  OUTSPIRAL (:SIDE+:INC) :INC :ANGLE
END
```

and some examples are given in Figures 4.6 to 4.10. These curves are closer to what most of us think are 'spirals', and those for angles of 60 degrees and 120 degrees correspond to familiar shapes. Figure 4.6 is the most spiral-like.

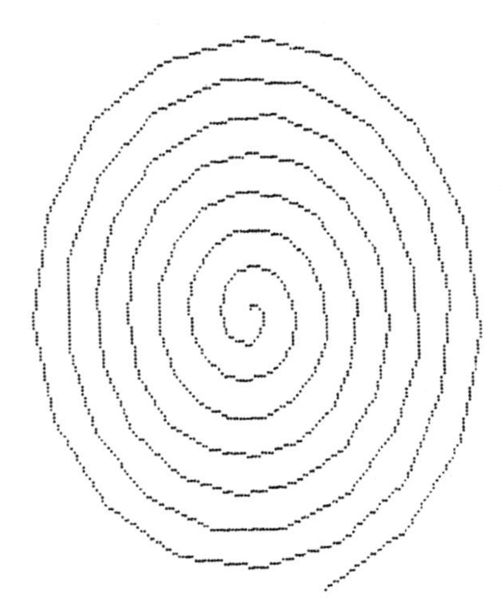

*Fig. 4.6.* OUTSPIRAL. :ANGLE=23.

*Fig. 4.7.* OUTSPIRAL. :ANGLE=60.

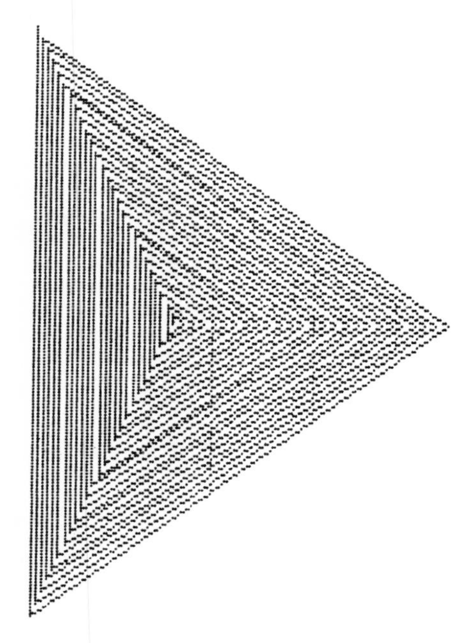

*Fig. 4.8.* OUTSPIRAL. :ANGLE=120.

*Fig. 4.9.* OUTSPIRAL. :ANGLE=117.

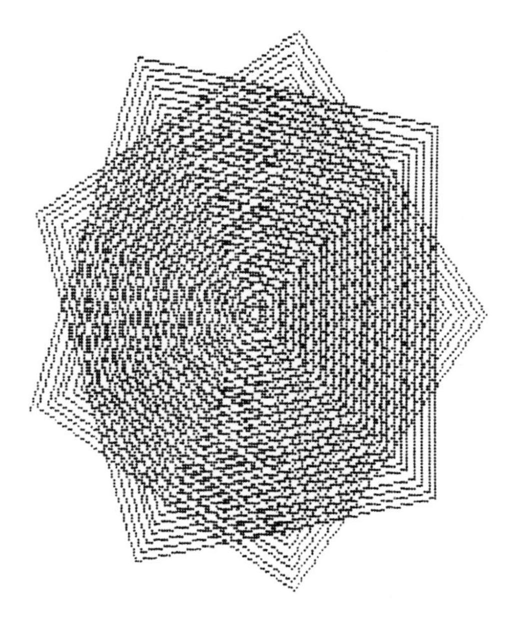

*Fig. 4.10.* OUTSPIRAL. :ANGLE=80.

With outward spirals the child has an opportunity to find out about prime numbers and factors. The child teaches himself to distinguish between those numbers/angles which give regular spirals (such as the angles 60, 72, 90 or 120) and numbers which produce less regular spirals (e.g. 117). Sooner or later (and often sooner) the child teaches himself to divide the angle into 360, to see if the result is a whole number.

Whole number results produce regular spirals. A regular spiral is produced when the angle is a factor of 360. One way to produce a very irregular spiral is to choose a large prime number, and the child discovers what are prime numbers by doing, rather than by listening.

How does OUTSPIRAL work? Let us try by calls,

```
CALL 1  OUTSPIRAL 10 2 117
CALL 2  OUTSPIRAL 12 2 117
CALL 3  OUTSPIRAL 14 2 117
CALL 4  OUTSPIRAL 16 2 117
CALL 5  OUTSPIRAL 18 2 117
CALL 6  OUTSPIRAL 20 2 117
```

For the result, see Figure 4.9. We can see that what happens is that the turns are regular, but the distance moved forward is steadily increased.

## A regular spiral

Figure 4.11 shows a special spiral, an inward spiral where the

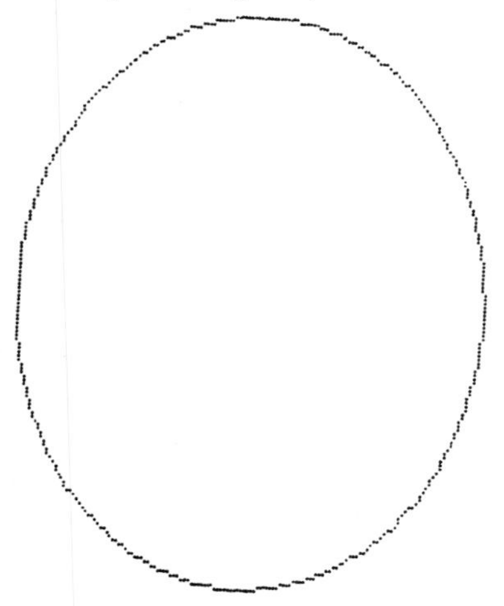

*Fig. 4.11.* INSPIRAL. :ANGLE=1 :INC=0.

starting angle is one degree, the size of each step is 50 units, and the increment to the angle is zero. The result is remarkably like a circle (though the printer routine used makes the circle look slightly squashed).

Figure 4.12 shows another circle, drawn by use of OUTSPIRAL.

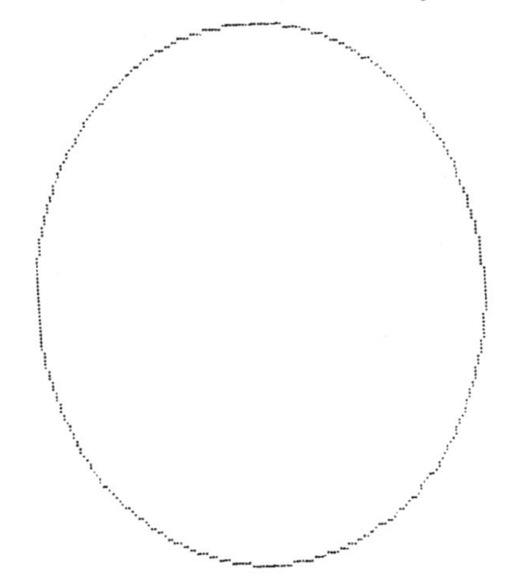

*Fig. 4.12.* OUTSPIRAL. :ANGLE=1 :INC=0.

In this case the angle is one, the initial length is 50, and the increment in length is zero. For the case where there are no increments, both procedures produce the same result – a circle. When an OUTSPIRAL meets an INSPIRAL we have a circle.

Isolating the common element of both procedures, when the increments are nil, we find that the key is the pair of moves

```
FORWARD :DISTANCE
RIGHT :ANGLE
```

repeated. The number of times we need to repeat the sequence depends on the value of ANGLE (i.e. :ANGLE). The child has to work out how the :ANGLE affects the number of repetitions. In this way they encounter the 'total trip theorem'.

Think of the turtle moving round the circle. Simulate (copy) the action in your mind, or walk round in a circle, or watch a turtle on the floor. To draw a circle by turning slightly, going forward, turning slightly, going forward ... means that the turtle turns full circle – the turtle turns through 360 degrees. The turtle always turns through 360 degrees, no matter what angle is provided for each turn.

If :ANGLE is 90 degrees, then a square is drawn, but the turtle (on its total trip) will go through 360 degrees (4 × 90 degrees). In MANYSIDES the reason why we had to turn through 120 degrees to draw an equilateral triangle was that the total trip had to be 360 degrees, and 120 = 360/3. An angle of 60 degrees produced a hexagon because 60 = 360/6.

A circle is really no more than a many-sided regular figure (it could be drawn by MANYSIDES with :TURN of 1). A procedure to draw a circle is

```
TO CIRCLE :SIDE
  REPEAT 360
    [FORWARD :SIDE RIGHT 1]
END
```

and this produces circles exactly like those in Figures 4.11 and 4.12. This is rather a slow way of drawing circles and, given the resolution of most LOGO graphics, rather too fine. (In Tandy Color LOGO, the above procedure – i.e. CIRCLE – will produce an octagon, because TCL cannot cope so well with fine distinctions in angles over small steps.)

## Polygon approximations

Here is a different procedure (which will not work in TI LOGO or TCL because those two work with whole numbers only):

```
TO POLYGON :ORDER :SIDE
  REPEAT :ORDER
    [FORWARD :SIDE/:ORDER
    RIGHT 360/:ORDER]
END
```

and the procedure draws polygons of :ORDER number of sides, where each side is :SIDE/:ORDER long.

Figure 4.13 is the result of

```
POLYGON 10 800 RIGHT 90
POLYGON 20 800 RIGHT 90
POLYGON 30 800 RIGHT 90
POLYGON 360 800 RIGHT 90
```

which shows that for most visual purposes a thirty-sided polygon looks like a circle. A child, who realises that a circle is little more

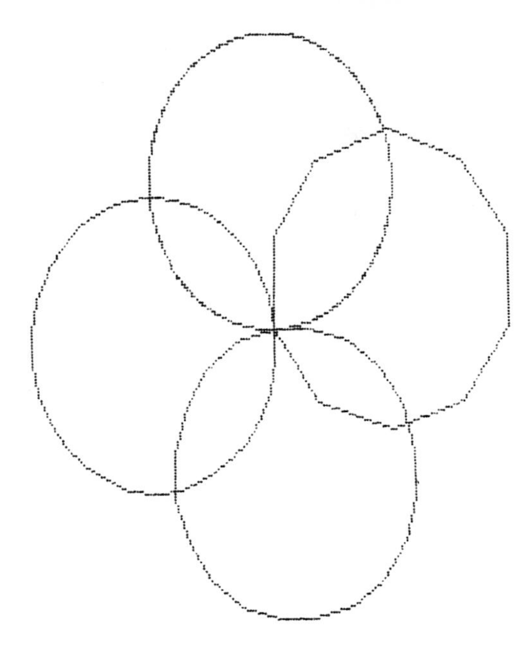

*Fig. 4.13.* Polygons.

than a series of many straight lines, has begun to use one of the most important ideas of mathematics.

It could be thought that this idea started with Zeno and his parable of Achilles and the Tortoise, and is the idea that the continuous is no more than the limit of the discrete. The continuous circle is no more than the limit of discrete polygons. If Seymour Papert had been English, he might have called his method Tortoise Geometry (the turtle is an American tortoise).

This powerful idea, and an idea many children soon grasp, reaches its heights of mathematical applicability in differential calculus. Children teach themselves to think naturally in terms of differential geometry, without realising that they are following in the footsteps of such giants as Newton and Leibniz.

Learning (teaching themselves) to draw circles in this manner, children realise that the curvature of a circle is constant at all points on its circumference. This highly abstract and conceptual point is hidden when the formula of a circle is given as $x^2 + y^2 = r^2$.

What else have they taught themselves? One very important point is that accuracy is a relative thing. A thirty-sided polygon is not a circle but it is close enough to be regarded as a good enough circle. 'Good enough' is antithetical to some approaches to learning, where there are right and wrong answers, and woe betide those who get the answer wrong! The'black and white' school of education is common in mathematics at all levels. LOGO presents mathematics as if it were a real, living subject and not some mystical holy writ. Though mathematics is used extensively in the sciences, mathematics is not a science. Mathematics is an art, a creative art.

Children teach themselves mathematics through a creative process, because in producing pictures on the display the child has to do something. The child is not being taught by a computer to answer fixed questions – the child is teaching the computer to do new things. Education is turned from the input of other people's information to the production of one's own information.

## The housing problem

One of Seymour Papert's most arresting examples is that of a child building a house. The house is as shown in Figure 4.14. The child (see *Mindstorms* pages 14–15) has a plan of the house – that in Figure 4.14, say – and has to decide how to draw the house. The child examines the whole and then the parts within the whole. The child sees a square and a triangle.

*Fig. 4.14.* A rough house.

Suppose there is a procedure SQUARE :SIDE which draws a square of :SIDE, and also suppose there is another procedure TRIANGLE :SIDE. The child's first attempt is

```
TO HOUSE :SIDE
  SQUARE :SIDE
  TRIANGLE :SIDE
END
```

which produces the result shown in Figure 4.15. It is an error, but not one to be treated too seriously. We have to establish why there was the error.

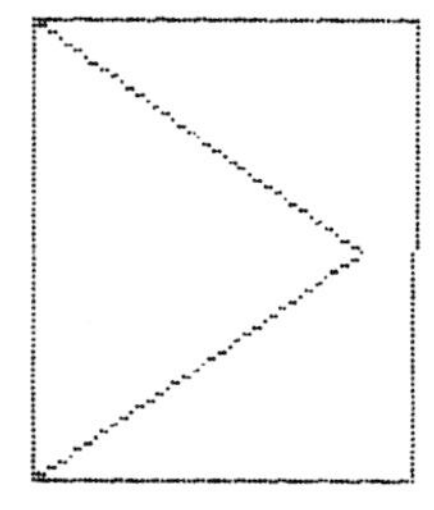

*Fig. 4.15.* A bugged house.

The error came because the square and the triangle started from the same point (bottom left) and both were turning in a circle clockwise – the total trip theorem.

We could sort this out at least two ways. Either we could tilt the whole triangle left through 60 degrees and then tilt the house; or we could move the whole triangle up the length of the house.

So, our alternative solutions are either

```
TO HOUSE :SIDE
  SQUARE :SIDE
  LEFT 60
  TRIANGLE :SIDE
END
```

to produce Figure 4.16, and then a slight modification to produce a PROPER.HOUSE

```
TO PROPER.HOUSE :SIDE
  RIGHT 90
  HOUSE :SIDE
END
```

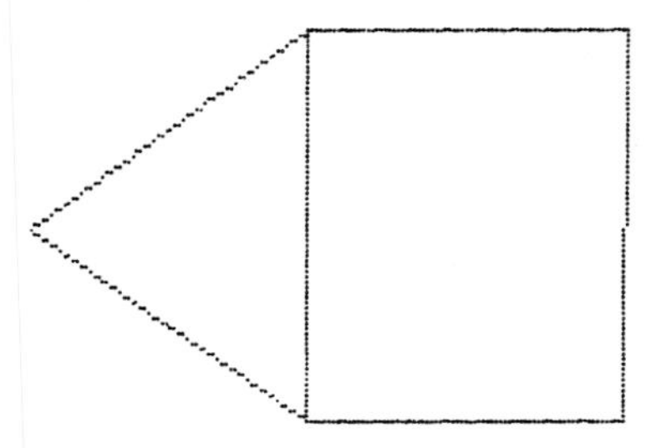

*Fig. 4.16.* A fallen house.

as in Figure 4.17. Or,

```
TO ANOTHER.HOUSE :SIDE
  SQUARE :SIDE
  PENUP
  FORWARD :SIDE
  PENDOWN
  RIGHT 30
  TRIANGLE :SIDE
END
```

will also result in the house drawn in Figure 4.17.

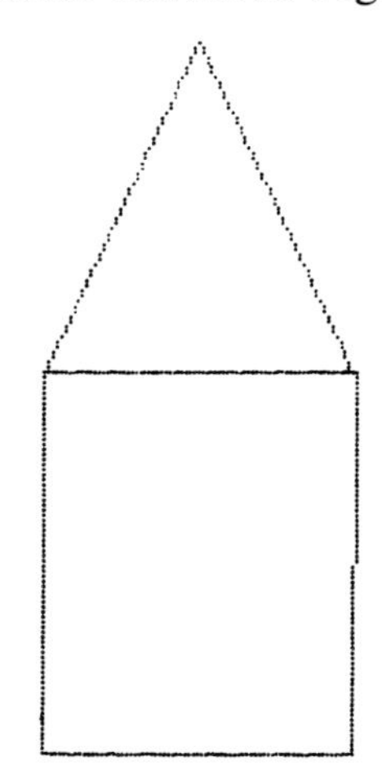

*Fig. 4.17.* A proper house.

The new command PENUP is an instruction to the mythical turtle to raise the pen it pulls along, so that when it moves it does not draw a line. PENDOWN means that the turtle then draws again. The two commands are not necessary, but I have used them to illustrate a useful facility. A child with an active mind will try to investigate the different ways in which triangle and square can be combined to produce a house. A line might be drawn, and the house tilted to be placed on the hill.

I tried this, and forgot that the house had to be tilted at 90 degrees to the hill. Figure 4.18 was the result – useful at a firework display,

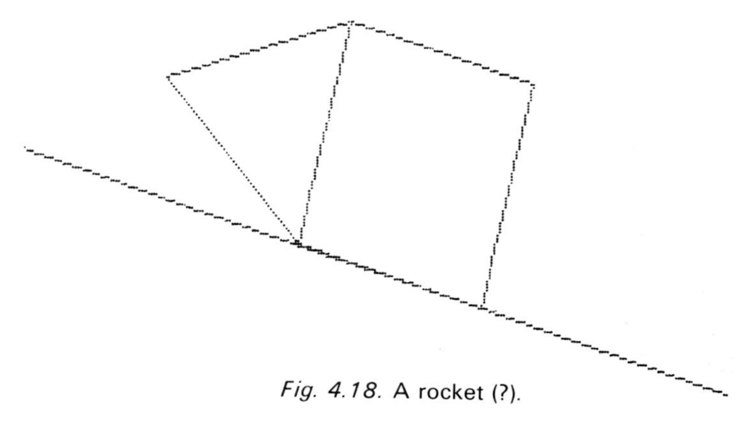

*Fig. 4.18.* A rocket (?).

but an inconvenient place in which to live. An extra turn right through 90 degrees gave the correct answer, that is, Figure 4.19. One learns by one's mistakes.

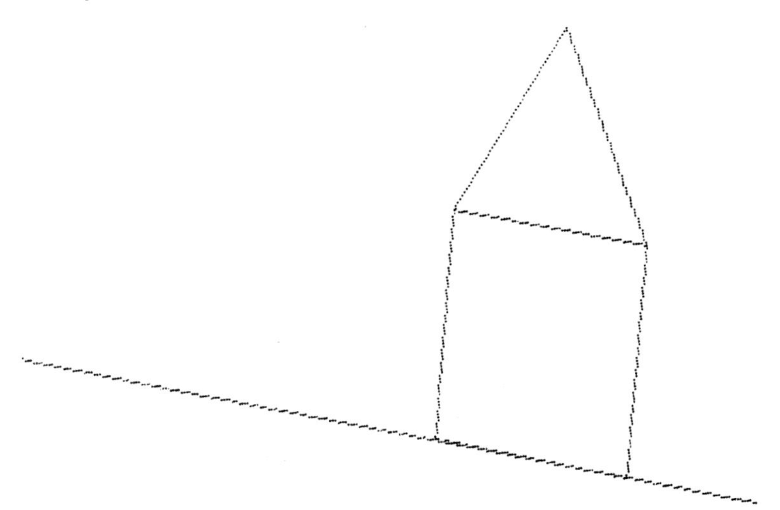

*Fig. 4.19.* A house on a hill.

An ingenious person might add a chimney with smoke. Smoke, remember, always goes straight up no matter what the house's inclination.

## Creative procedures

It is worth considering what is the difference between recursive procedures and non-recursive procedures (those, for example, which use REPEAT). When we were drawing the circles by use of the spiral procedures, the drawing was by use of a recursive procedure. Both INSPIRAL and OUTSPIRAL refer to themselves within the body of the routine.

The spiral procedures were rather more general than the circle procedure, or the polygon procedures, and by allowing the procedure to continue without stopping there were no limits upon the progress of the procedure. When we knew what had to be done, we were able to be more deterministic – we could say how many times an action was to be performed.

With LOGO's powerful use of procedures (whether they are recursive, or use REPEAT) the user of LOGO is able to exercise that highly important, but sadly underused, faculty of imagination. Though the teacher may assist at times, the true teacher of the child is the child. The child is teaching himself when he is at work creating effects, by developing new procedures, to extend his own information base. Papert would say that the child is creating his own *microworld*.

It is of note that, though I have called the child by the conventional 'he', girls seem to benefit more from using LOGO than do boys. Boys are not held back by LOGO, but girls seem to be able to teach themselves more by using LOGO. Perhaps this is because girls are more creative and respond to the challenge in LOGO – but, then, who knows?

# Chapter Five
# Arithmetical LOGO

A mathematician, like a painter or a poet, is a maker of patterns. If his patterns are more permanent than theirs, it is because they are made with ideas.

*A Mathematician's Apology* by G H Hardy

To add two numbers together, and store the result in a variable, is simple to perform in most LOGOs. Thus,

```
MAKE "VAR 3+4
```

and the value stored in VAR is now 7. In Research Machines LOGO, this line looks rather different:

```
MAKE 'VAR ADD 3   4
```

and the difference is rather important.

## Prefix and infix

In the first example of addition the key operation is +, which is fixed in between the two numbers. The plus sign is an *infix* operator, and conventionally (in arithmetic) most operators are infix. Versions of LOGO which come from Seymour Papert's home institution of MIT tend to use the conventional infix notation.

In the second example the key operation is ADD, which precedes the two numbers on which it operates. ADD is a *prefix* operator, and only one version of LOGO exclusively uses this form: that which comes from the Department of Artificial Intelligence at Edinburgh University.

The MIT versions derive very clearly from the Papert philosophy of the child directing the computer, with very little assistance from adults. MIT versions (in which are included versions for computers from the Apple to the Spectrum) are all intended to assist in the development of the individual.

The Edinburgh versions follow a different, less radical philosophy. The Edinburgh versions are seen as being used in more conventional, more teacher-directed environments, with far more emphasis on 'planning' in an older sense than there is on 'creation' in a newer sense. LOGO, in the Edinburgh version, follows LISP (an artificial intelligence language) far more closely than does any other version.

At MIT, LOGO took many ideas – especially those concerned with analysing lists – from LISP, which was another MIT language (invented by John McCarthy, it stands for 'LISt Processing language'). In the way in which LOGO was developed by Seymour Papert and his co-workers, it did not take on board many of the other LISP features, such as the exclusive use of prefix operators. Edinburgh versions make LOGO appear as if it were a version of LISP with the addition of turtle graphics.

To add together two numbers in LISP, and then to store the result in a variable, we write (depending on versions):

```
(SETQ VAR (PLUS 3   4))
```

and the correspondence with the Edinburgh version of LOGO is clear to see. All we need do is to change SETQ to MAKE, PLUS to ADD, and ignore the brackets: they are then the same. There are some advantages to the prefix method, in that its supporters claim that the prefix method is much more inherently logical and, therefore, clear. In fact, many LOGOS have both systems at once.

Suppose we wrote, in an MIT version,

```
MAKE "VAR 3   -4
```

with a space between the 3 and the minus sign. Do we mean that :VAR is to be 3, and −4 is for something else? Do we mean :VAR is −1? Is the space important, or is it just there by accident, for no reason? Note that

```
MAKE "VAR (3   -4)
```

is not ambiguous, which is why I have used this method for collecting terms together.

In Waterloo LOGO (for the IBM PC), there are two forms of minus sign:

```
3  -4
```

means −1, whereas

3 ~ 4

means 3 and −4. The ~ (tilde) is a 'unary' minus. It does not mean subtract, it just means that this is a minus number. In this LOGO, 3 −4 (wherever the spaces) is always −1 and 3 ~ 4 is always 3 and −4. There is no unary plus in Waterloo LOGO because we usually write 3 4 when we mean 3 and 4, and rarely write 3 +4.

Consider the following RML line of program:

```
PRINT MULTIPLY ADD 1 2 ADD 2 DIVIDE 10 5
>> 12
```

and compare it to a more conventional LOGO form:

```
PRINT (1+2)*(2+10/2)
>> 12
```

and then to the equivalent line of LISP (note that LISP is integer only)

```
PRINT (TIMES (PLUS 1 2) (PLUS 2 (QUOTIENT 10 5))))
>> 12
```

LISP is certainly the most confusing version of the three for the uninitiated. For most people the MIT version makes most sense.

## Planning versus creativity

The LOGO developed at Edinburgh is the result of a fairly small research project (involving only forty children of average ability between the ages of 12–15 years). Given the small number of children, and given that those involved in the research project came from a department of Artificial Intelligence, perhaps the influence of LISP is not strange.

The MIT LOGOs have been researched on a far greater number of children, in many more differing environments, than the Edinburgh style of LOGO. This is one reason why I think that the MIT versions are superior: they have been tried with many more children, in a wider range of environments, than has the Edinburgh version.

Another reason why I believe that the MIT versions are conceptually superior to the Edinburgh version is that I believe the MIT view of the place of LOGO in education is the correct view.

Seymour Papert and his co-workers see LOGO as an exercise in which children are the directors of their own work, they work in their own way, at their own pace. What the child learns, and in what order, partly depends on the child, and partly depends on the suggestions, hints, and clues which others provide. In the Papert vision, the 'others' are as likely to be other children and, in fact, are even more likely to be other children than they are to be adults.

At Edinburgh, the approach contravened the true spirit of the free-wheeling LOGO philosophy from MIT. The Edinburgh team used LOGO within a conventional class situation, with the intent to teach specific topics in a specific order. In this style the child has to follow a set pattern of topics, rather than the child creating his own way through his own topics. Edinburgh LOGO is rather more staid in its intent than the intentionally radical MIT LOGOs.

As those at Edinburgh did not want to cause confusion over the meaning of spaces, they set up a very firm (highly LISP derivative) way of expressing what was to be done. As there might be confusion over the meaning of '3 −4', for example, this was forbidden by the Edinburgh dialect of LOGO.

The Edinburgh version seems to be going back to the 'no errors here' attitude towards education. This is more than slightly unfortunate, as this is the version available on Research Machines, and many schools in Britain already have RML machines.

The philosophy which underpins Edinburgh LOGO means that it is not the best version to use. In my opinion, Edinburgh LOGO needs to be tried out on many more children, and improved as a result.

## An arithmetical procedure

I make no apologies for the choice of my first example. This is an example which is so frequently used to demonstrate arithmetical programming that the expert will yawn when I say it is the 'factorial'. It is, however, a very good example, particularly if we are also examining the differences in LOGO philosophies.

The factorial of the variable N is defined is being $1 \times 2 \times 3 \times \ldots \times (N-1) \times N$. In some computer languages, with facilities for loops, the factorial is most easily calculated as the product of the successive values of the loop counter. LOGO does not have a loop facility, so what do we do?

The factorial of 1 is 1, that of 2 is 2, that of 3 is 6, and the factorial of 4 is 24. The factorial of N+1, it would seem, is equal to N+1 times the factorial of N. If we set the factorial of 0 equal to 1, and disallow any negative values, then the progression works.

The calculation of the factorial seems rather recursive. Here is an attempt in a normal (i.e. MIT) LOGO

```
TO FACT :N
  IF :N < 1 THEN OUTPUT 1
    ELSE OUTPUT :N*:FACT :N-1
END
```

where the IF line is typed in as one physical line on the computer. The new command OUTPUT means that the evaluation of the procedure is stopped at that point, and the value returned by the procedure is that which follows OUTPUT.

This should work for most MIT-based LOGOs, even if it is an integer-only LOGO (other than TCL). In RML LOGO we might enter

```
BUILD FACT :N
  IF LESSQ :N 1 THEN RESULT 1 ELSE
    RESULT MULTIPLY :N FACT SUBTRACT :N 1
END
```

and this confusing method of presentation is why I will ignore RML LOGO in the rest of this chapter.

A further way of writing this version of the factorial, for Apple LOGO, is

```
TO FACT :N
  TEST :N < 1
  IFTRUE OUTPUT 1
  IFFALSE OUTPUT :N*FACT :N-1
END
```

This is another Apple LOGO version of the IF THEN ELSE.

The factorial will not be calculated if the input is not a number (e.g. if a person enters 'five'). It will work, but not give the correct answer, if the input is not an integer. (The equivalent of the factorial for non-integer values is the gamma function.) We will ignore the possibility of non-numerical input, but will allow the possibility of a non-integer input – though if the user is the person who has created the procedure, it is not a likely error.

The revised procedure is

```
TO FACT :N
  IF NOT (INTEGER :N = :N) THEN STOP
  IF :N < 1 THEN OUTPUT
    ELSE OUTPUT :N*FACT :N-1
END
```

and the extra line says that if the integer part of the number is not equal to the number (i.e. it is not an integer) then stop evaluating the procedure.

## A function graph

Why not draw a graph of the factorial? To draw a graph all we need to do is to connect some points by using the turtle. Sounds simple?

To fix the points to which the turtle is to move in its journey, we use

```
SETPOS [ :X :Y ]
```

and this command moves the turtle to those absolute coordinates, as given by the two elements in the list. If we wish to move to coordinates 30 and 40, then we enter

```
SETPOS SENTENCE 30  40
```

or

```
SETPOS [30 40]
```

The new command SENTENCE takes the two inputs and turns them into a list – and SETPOS expects a list. SETPOS is an Apple LOGO command, and other versions of LOGO have different versions of the command. Many of the other versions do not have a list as input, but I will use Apple LOGO because we learn through its use of SENTENCE.

Let us start. The first procedure will draw the graph, for values of the number from 1 to 7,

```
TO GRAPH
  LOCAL "X "Y
  MAKE "X 0
  REPEAT 7[MAKE "X :X+1 MAKE "Y FACT :X
    SETPOS SENTENCE :X*10 :Y/7]
END
```

and this is all that is required.

The variables X and Y are defined as LOCAL to that procedure: this means that if we have defined X and Y in some other procedure, the two sets will not be confused. X is given the starting value 0.

The next portion is repeated 7 times, X is made larger by 1, and Y is made equal to the value of the factorial of X. The turtle is moved to the value of X times 10, and to the value of Y divided by 7. End of graph routine.

## Common Denominators

Take two integers, say 48 and 30. We need to find what is the greatest common denominator, that is, which number is the largest number which will divide exactly into 48 and 30. The answer is, of course, 6.

Suppose we wish to mechanise the process, how shall we proceed? Obviously one way to proceed is to take all the numbers from 1 upwards, and successively divide the numbers into 48 and 30, until we find the largest number which will divide exactly into them both. Seems rather complex, really, because we will have to keep a check on what was the largest number until we have finished.

Try to think how we can simplify matters. If the largest common denominator is 6, it will also divide into 48–30 = 18. It is this simple fact which gives an exceedingly easy way to calculate the greatest common denominator.

If the GCD (greatest common denominator) divides into 18, 30, and 48, it must also divide into 30–18 = 12. The GCD must also divide into 18–12 = 6, and then 12–6 = 6. When we reach the stage 6–6 = 0, we know we have solved the problem, the GCD is 6.

Try another set of numbers. Imagine a child has been introduced to the GCD method, and then has to decide what to do with that method. The numbers are 96 and 30.96–30=66 which is still greater than 30, so 66–30=36, and then 36–30=6. Another way of arriving at 6 is to try 96 MODULO 30, that is, the remainder given when 96 is divided by 30. The remainder when 30 is divided by 6 is 0, and so when the remainder is zero, we know the divisor is the GCD.

A final example we can try is 21 and 8. Set it out as a sequence

| | | |
|---|---|---|
| 21 | 8 | |
| 8 | 5 | (21 MOD 8) |
| 5 | 3 | (8 MOD 5) |

```
3       2       (5 MOD 3)
2       1       (3 MOD 2)
1       0       (2 MOD 1)
```

and the greatest common divisor of 21 and 8 is 1. To define the routine we will try:

```
TO GCD :BIGGER :SMALLER
  IF :SMALLER = 0 THEN OUTPUT :BIGGER
    ELSE OUTPUT GCD :SMALLER
      REMAINDER :BIGGER :SMALLER
END
```

and this will work well, as long as :BIGGER is greater than :SMALLER – but what if it is not?

We need to have some facility to exchange values, if it is necessary. We can define another procedure to cope with this problem:

```
TO GCD2 :N1 :N2
  IF :N1 > :N1 THEN GCD :N1 :N2
    ELSE GCD :N2 :N1
END
```

though it would be possible to incorporate such a check in GCD this makes the sequence clearer. The check on the size of the numbers is only needed once, because the remainder must be less than the divisor.

The lowest common multiple is that number which is the smallest number into which both numbers divide exactly. The LCM is related to the GCD by the simple arithmetical expression:

```
:NUMBER1*:NUMBER2/(GCD2 :NUMBER1 :NUMBER2)
```

so the LCM is defined by

```
TO LCM :N1 :N2
  OUTPUT :N1*:N2/(GCD2 :N1 :N2)
END
```

This shows how we can create a package of little procedures to investigate elementary number theory, to be related with some of the work on spirals.

In some LOGOs, we are able to create 'packages' which are then separate entities. These packages are then treated as entities for storage or erasure. In Apple LOGO, for example,

```
PACKAGE "NUMBER. THEORY "GCD "GCD2 "LCM
```

would put the above routines into the package NUMBER. THEORY. The package can be protected from accidental erasure and interference by using BURY "NUMBER.THEORY, which allows the routines to be used, but not to be altered. (Its reverse is UNBURY.)

## Numbers

As I noted earlier, the size of the factorial rapidly increases. The factorial of 11 is already 39916800, a number of eight digits.

In RML LOGO it is only possible to have an accuracy of seven digits, so that 39916800 and 39916802 will both be shown as 39916800. TI LOGO and TCL both only allow integers in the range – 32768 to 32767, so it can be seen that there are no simple absolutes here either.

Both Apple LOGO and Terrapin LOGO allow integers in the range −2147483648 to +214783648, and the calculation of the factorial would be treated as an integer calculation. If, however, .1 was added to 39916800 the result would be a real (i.e. fractional) number, and fractional numbers are only stored to an accuracy of seven digits.

The number 39916800, as a real number, is shown as 3.99168E7 in these latter two LOGOs, and −39916800, as a real number, is shown as −3.99168E7. The number.0000000001 is shown as 1N10 where the N stands for a negative exponent (i.e. a number less than 1). 1N10 might be thought to be the equivalent of the invalid form 1E–10.

Though it might be thought that the accuracy for real numbers of Terrapin and Apple LOGOs is good (about 1N38 to 1E38), neither can stand comparison with the accuracy of Waterloo LOGO for the IBM PC. All Waterloo LOGO arithmetic is performed using decimal floating-point with 12 digits of precision (greater than the integer precision of the others).

The size of the exponent varies from 1E ~16384 to 1E16383, and so in this version N is not used, rather E and the special ~ sign for unary minus. To show that this extreme accuracy is perhaps rather wasted, it is worth remembering that the total number of electrons in the universe is 1E79.

## Operating with numbers

As some LOGOs do not allow fractional arithmetic (especially TCL and TI LOGO) these LOGOs tend to have the simplest procedures for dealing with numbers. Both go little beyond the four rules of number, plus a facility to produce random numbers.

LOGOs with fractional capabilities usually have trigonometrical ratios as well, though RML does not have an arctangent. (The arctangent is used for working out angles, when you know the distances.) Most also have a square root facility.

Suppose we have two sides of a triangle, the included angle, and wish to find the length of the remaining side. We use the cosine rule $A^2 = B^2 + C^2 - 2BC\cos(a)$. As a LOGO procedure it might look like

```
TO OTHER.SIDE :B :C :A
  OUTPUT :B*:B+:C*:C-2*:B*:C*COS :A
END
```

We could use, for example:

```
MAKE “C.SIDE OTHER.SIDE 30 20 23
```

where we have two sides of 30 and 20, with an included angle of 23. The other side is now given by :C.SIDE.

The omission of the arctangent in RML LOGO is very strange. It possibly reflects on its parentage, in that Edinburgh LOGOs are not designed to be as widely extensible as the MIT versions.

Simple playing with numbers can be seen by some as an end in itself, but usually it is a means to an end, e.g. graphics, which is discussed in the next chapter.

Chapter Six
# Geometrical LOGO

Men are like trees: each one must put forth the leaf that is created in him.

*Proverbs from Plymouth Pulpit* by Henry Ward Beecher

The turtle sits on the graphics screen. It can move forward, it can move back, it can turn. The turtle can draw lines with its pen down, it just moves when its pen is up. End of story.

The turtle is a parochial animal, in that it does not care what is happening anywhere else, all that it does is plough its furrow regardless. When the turtle is drawing a circle it does not know, or care, where the centre of the circle is. All the turtle does is go forward a certain distance, and then turn through a certain number of degrees.

We know where the centre is, but we draw the circle by starting the turtle somewhere on the circumference of the circle. We have to work out where the circumference is situated, and how far forward each little move has to be. To establish that information requires the use of some trigonometry.

## The screen

Normally the turtle starts in the middle of the screen, pointing directly upwards. The coordinates at the centre are usually 0,0 where the X axis is horizontal and the Y axis is vertical. Angles are measured clockwise with 0 being directly upwards.

These are the normal characteristics of most MIT LOGOs (except TCL for which the origin is bottom left), but for an Edinburgh LOGO the origin is bottom left and the angle increases in a counter-clockwise direction from a zero direction pointing right. The

Edinburgh formulation is that of traditional mathematics (especially the counter-clockwise measurement of angle).

Personally, I prefer a system in which the origin is at the centre, the turtle points straight upwards, and the angles increase in a counter-clockwise direction. No LOGO follows this formulation, as far as I am aware. Different LOGOs have differing resolutions, that is, the 'width' and 'breadth' of the coordinates, but most are effectively the same (approximately 256 by 192, though there are variations).

Some of the newest, and most interesting, aspects of LOGOs are those which come from the use of *sprites* (e.g. TI LOGO, Atari LOGO, and Commodore 64 LOGO), or multiple turtles (e.g. TCL). A sprite is a special type of programmable shape which can be displayed anywhere on the screen. All the user has to do is to tell a sprite what shape it is, what colour it is, and where it has to go. On the Commodore 64 and the TI 99/4A, the sprites are controlled by a special chip within the computer. On the Atari, they are called 'demons' and they are controlled only by the software.

'Proper' sprites are produced by special hardware facilities; they have a direction and a speed, but they do not affect the normal graphics. Sprites add continuous movement to the discrete moves of the turtle. The potential of sprites in the teaching of science (especially dynamics) is great, and they are very much in the true LOGO philosophy of extending the language where possible to incorporate new, and useful, features of computers.

Sprites in TI LOGO have special variables such as SPEED (which can be resolved into the velocities in the X and Y directions, XVEL and YVEL), and the velocity can be set by SETSPEED. A sprite can CARRY a previously defined shape, or one can be defined by MAKESHAPE. Thus it continues.

## The tree

There are so many small variations in the way LOGOs describe their operation. I will, therefore, give an idealised version of LOGO, in the following routines, in which the main intent is to clarify what is happening.

Look at Figure 6.1. It is a picture of a V, the angle between the two lines is 90 degrees, and it is supposed to be symmetrical. Now look at Figure 6.2, which is Figure 6.1 with another Figure 6.1 at each end of the lines. When we reach Figure 6.6, the picture is rather more complex looking, but we know that it is no more than a series of Figures 6.1.

*Fig. 6.1.* Tree 1.

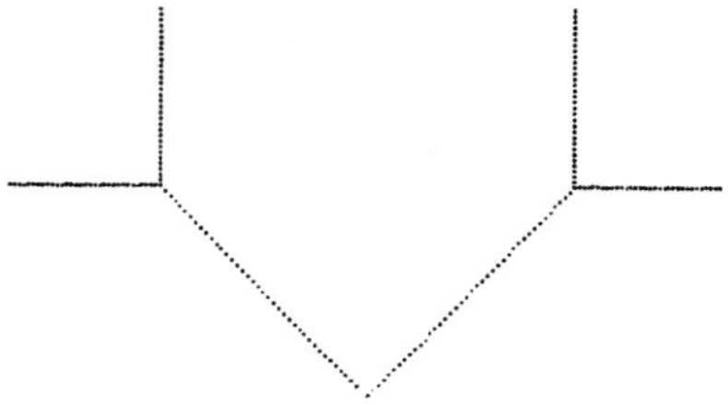

*Fig. 6.2.* Tree 2.

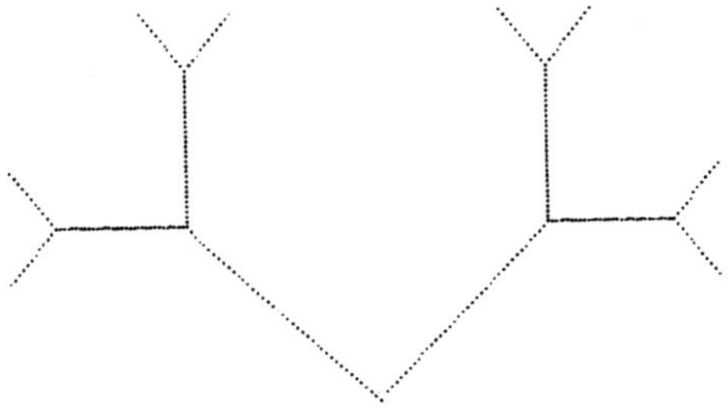

*Fig. 6.3.* Tree 3.

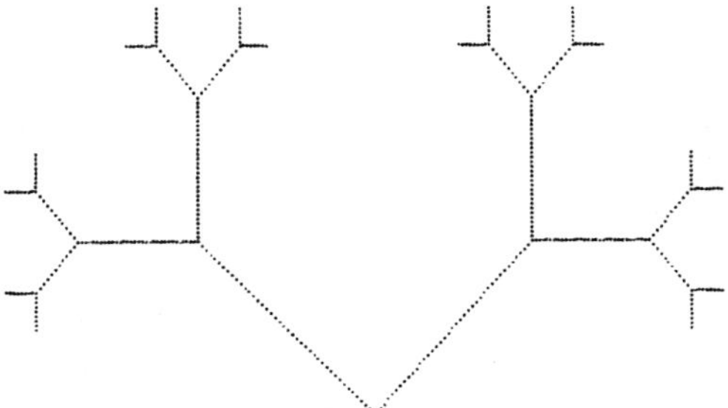

*Fig. 6.4.* Tree 4.

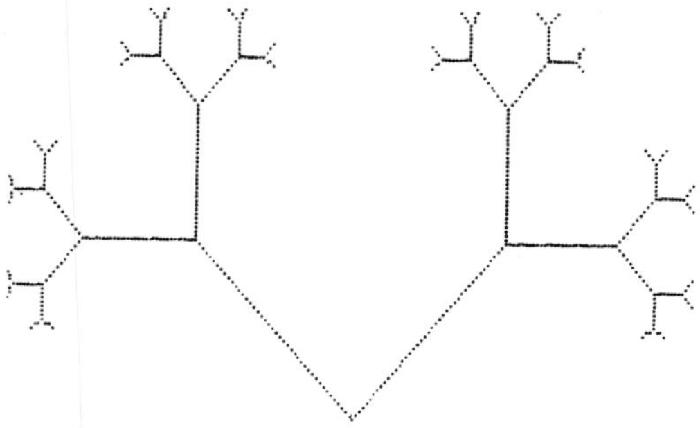

*Fig. 6.5.* Tree 5.

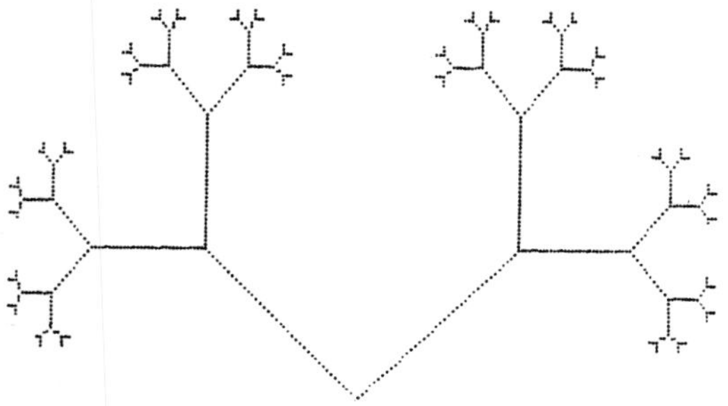

*Fig. 6.6.* Tree 6.

This 'tree' obviously has recursive leanings (some later trees lean rather more than these). The procedure is:

```
TO TREE :LENGTH :ORDER
  IF :ORDER = 0 THEN [STOP]
  LEFT 45
  FORWARD :LENGTH
  TREE :LENGTH/2 :ORDER-1
  PENUP
  BACK :LENGTH
  RIGHT 90
  PENDOWN
  FORWARD :LENGTH
  TREE :LENGTH/2 :ORDER-1
  PENUP
  BACK :LENGTH
  LEFT 45
  PENDOWN
END
```

Start by considering how it relates to Figure 6.1. Ignore for the moment the relevance of :ORDER and the recursive calls to TREE. First (ignoring all lines with :ORDER) the turtle turns left through 45 degrees. As originally it is pointing upwards, this means that it now points left 45 degrees from the vertical. The turtle is now instructed to move forward :LENGTH units. Now we have drawn the line on the left.

The pen is raised, so the turtle does not draw, and it travels backwards (i.e. still facing in the same direction), the distance :LENGTH. It is now, therefore, back where it started. It still faces 45 degrees left from the vertical.

The pen is lowered after a turn right through 90 degrees. This means that the turtle now faces 45 degrees right from the vertical. A line :LENGTH units long is drawn, the pen raised and the turtle goes back to the start. A turn is made left through 45 degrees, to bring back the turtle to its starting point, and the pen is lowered.

Ignoring the commands with :ORDER, the turtle draws two lines, and then ends back where it started, pointing in the same direction.

Now to consider the second parameter, :ORDER. If the value of ORDER is 0, then the procedure goes no further, otherwise it draws the line at 45 degrees to the vertical. When the end of the line is reached, the procedure TREE is again activated.

TREE is now activated with the length of line halved, and the order reduced by 1. At that moment the turtle is pointing in the direction of the line, and so the next call of TREE will be symmetrical on either side of that direction, as long as :ORDER–1 is not zero. This is Figure 6.2. As the original parameter :ORDER is increased, the complexity of the tree increases.

Figure 6.7 shows the result of using a very large value of ORDER, in this case 10. The final value of :LENGTH after ten halvings is

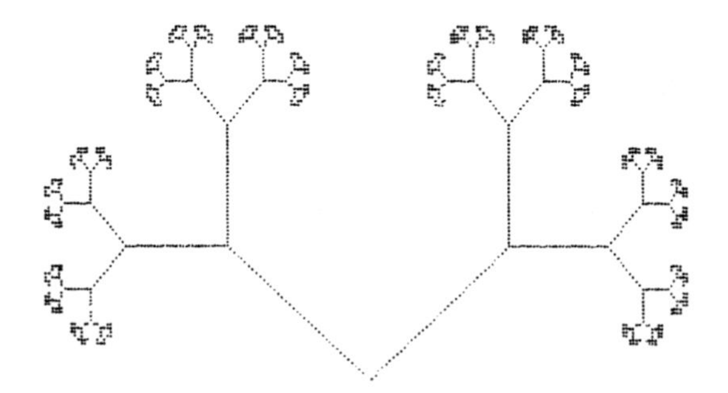

*Fig. 6.7.* Tree 10.

about a thousand times smaller than the original value, and so the little increments are not drawn. Figure 6.7 could be said to be the final shape of the tree; increasing the order will have no effect.

For these pictures I am using a computer with a very high resolution, and special routines. Normally such detail cannot be obtained.

## A learning tree

The tree so far calculated is a boring, though possibly pretty, tree. Even such a mundane little tree can have its uses, because it is on trees such as this that many searches are based. Note that the tree in Figure 6.7 has 1024 branch endings.

Start by considering how one can discover a hidden number between 0 and 127, when the only information available is answers to the question whether to go higher or to go lower. Think of a number.

I guess 64, and you tell me that it is higher. The base of the tree is 64. I will consider high numbers to be on the right side of the tree, so you have told me to investigate the right hand portion. My next guess is 96, because the next node is 96 (mid-way between 64 and 127). You tell me to go lower, and so I know the number must be between 64 and 96, the left branch from the 96 node.

I keep on making guesses in the same manner, following the same rules, and slowly we traverse the tree, searching for illumination and truth. When we have traversed seven nodes, we have the answer. Each branch ending has a number, and the search is to find the correct branch end. We only need seven nodes, or a tree where :ORDER = 7, to arrive at a solution because 2*2*2*2*2*2*2 = 128, and we have 128 different possibilities.

In the radio game *Twenty Questions* the panel are allowed twenty questions, which are answered yes or no. Twenty 2s ($2^{20}$) multiplied together make 1Ø48576, and so in this game the panelists can sift through over one million different facts – assuming that they ask questions which are sufficiently different to count as different questions. Sometimes they even get a little help.

Showing the progress of a session of questions, by using a tree the child has constructed, is one place where an aware teacher can be invaluable.

Another useful item to be learnt from the tree is how the discrete tends to the continuous. The lengths of successive branches follow a geometrical ratio (the ratio in changing sizes is constant), and children can see visually that the summation of a geometrical ratio is a constant, to which the summation approaches.

The tree with order 10 is sufficient to convince most children that that is almost where it will end. If the children try to use a higher order tree, they will find that the time taken increases greatly. They will also find that the result is no different from what they would have obtained from a lower order. Just as with the circle, we do not have to draw a perfect shape to obtain a close enough approximation.

Instead of dividing by 2 we can divide by other numbers, and find that if the number by which we divide is less than 1 then the tree stops growing outwards. To investigate such summation simulations we can adapt the TREE to produce TREE2:

```
TO TREE2 :LENGTH :ORDER :FACTOR
  TREE2 :LENGTH/:FACTOR :ORDER-1 :FACTOR
  ...
END
```

Here most of the procedure is similar to TREE, except for the parameters and the procedure calls. If :FACTOR is equal to 1 or is greater, then the tree just gets bigger and bigger.

If a procedure is produced which varies :FACTOR so that it goes in the progression 1, 2, 3, 4, onwards, then it will be found that the tree steadily increases in size without stopping (the harmonic series, which slowly sums to infinity). The tree can be quite productive at the secondary school level, or even higher.

## A Leaning Tree

It has to be admitted, though, that the binary tree is boring ('binary'

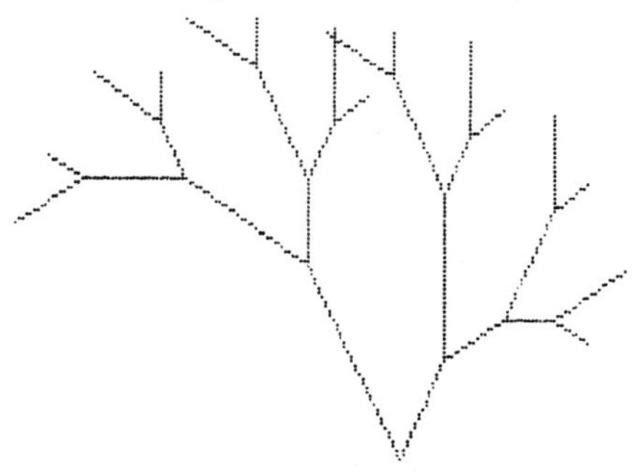

*Fig. 6.8.* Leaning tree 1.

in this sense means 'of two possible values'). It is so sensible, so predictable, so useful, so boring. Why must the tree be so upright? Why not have different branch ratios. Is not the tree in Figure 6.8 much prettier?

In the tree in Figure 6.8, those branches on the left are relatively longer than those on the right, and the angle between the branches is also not 90 degrees. This tree looks more complicated, but it is not.

```
TO LEAN.TREE :L :A :O :F1 :F2
   IF :O= 0 THEN [STOP]
   LEFT :A
   FORWARD :L
   LEAN.TREE :L*:F1 :A :O-1 :F1 :F2
   PENUP
   BACK :L
   RIGHT 2*:A
   PENDOWN
   FORWARD :L*:F2
   LEAN.TREE :L*:F1 :A :O-1 :F1 :F2
   PENUP
   BACK :L*F2
   LEFT :A
   PENDOWN
END
```

The most important item to notice about this procedure is the use of two factors :F1, and :F2. The first sets the size of corresponding branches from call to call; and the second sets the relative size of the branches within the call. The angle :A also gives a measure of the spread of the tree.

Figures 6.8 to 6.11 show the effects of using different values for

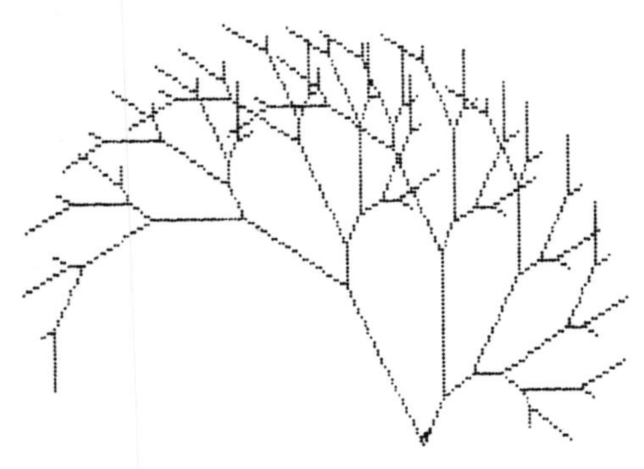

*Fig. 6.9.* Leaning tree 2.

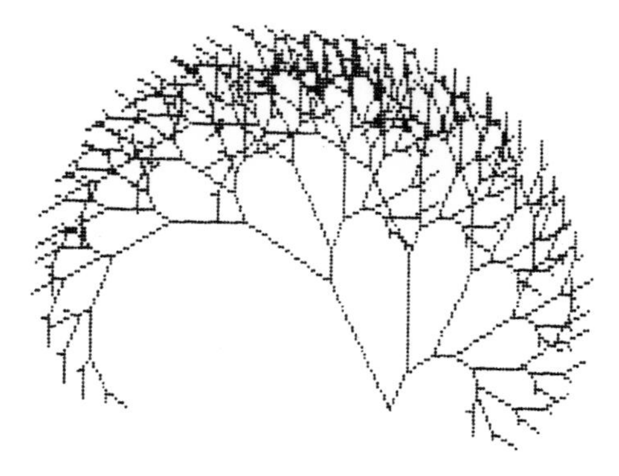

*Fig. 6.10.* Leaning tree 3.

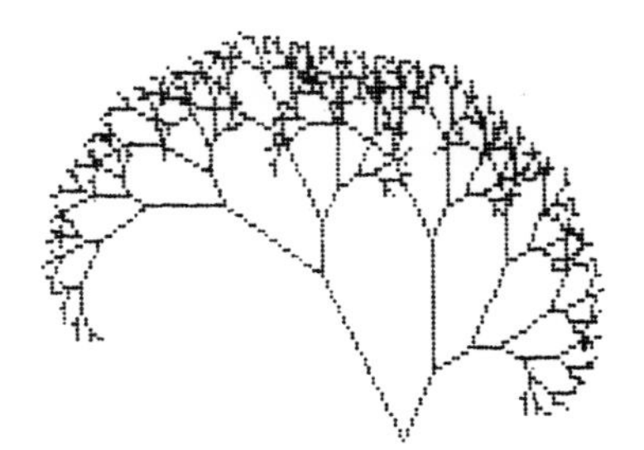

*Fig. 6.11.* Leaning tree 4.

these parameters. Figure 6.10 is possibly the most interesting, because it is the tree which creeps round the corner. This figure shows again the way in which limits are reached (there is a nice curve around the foliage).

Figure 6.10 also shows how the disparity between the lengths of left and right branches, and the resulting differing degrees of curvature, affect shapes. If the foliage is examined, blobs can be seen. The blobs are not part of the design, they are a part of the way the screen of the computer implements its graphics.

Looking carefully at the edge of the foliage, straight lines may be discerned, and the edges have a slight flattening, particularly at the top. This flattening, and angularity, is possibly clearest in the case of Figure 6.11. The straightness is implicit in all the other leaning trees but can be most clearly seen here.

The shapes we can draw by LEAN.TREE also match the growth processes of plants and trees in nature. Under the influence of a prevailing wind (from, say, the right) branches to the right will be restricted in their length compared to those branches pointing to the left. Figure 6.8 is probably the clearest example of this phenomenon, and all the other trees are exaggerated versions of this basic pattern.

These kinds of illustrations have many interesting biological consequences. It is easy to see how snail shells, seed heads, animal horns, and many other similar phenomena can be investigated very simply. This is also work which has relevance at higher levels of education, and in fact the tree procedures are based on ideas presented in *Patterns in Nature* by Peter S. Stevens (1974).

## Interference patterns

We have a procedure:

```
TO CIRCLE :INC
  REPEAT 20 [FORWARD :INC RIGHT 18]
END
```

and it draws a circle of 20 sides. That is, we approximate a circle by a polygon of 20 sides, and each side is of length :INC.

This is a fairly standard procedure, and we could, if we wished, modify it to accommodate a specific radius, but I want to use it to show how the video display on the computer can interact with the patterns we draw. Already we have seen one effect, for we can draw a circle with 20 sides and it looks fine.

The display on most computer graphics systems is split, visually, into small rectangles called 'pixels'. Any one pixel can either be one colour or another. Part of the pixel cannot be black and another part white; it is either all black or all white. What happens, then, when we draw a line?

Find some tiles on the floor, or use a piece of graph paper, and then draw a straight line. The line is a line, but if the line is at any angle to the orientation of the tiles the lines will be ragged. Whenever a line goes through a tile, that tile is coloured black (perhaps only in the mind) but, when looking at those black tiles, it is easy to see that the black tiles do not make a black line. The line has kinks as we move from one line of tiles to another line.

If you go back through some of the earlier figures (of squares and similar) you will see strange little kinks in lines where there should not be a kink. Though on the one hand this might seem annoying, it can lead to some interesting effects. This is why we want to CIRCLE.

We use CIRCLE in this procedure:

```
TO INTERCIRCLE
  LOCAL "INC
  MAKE "INC 0
  REPEAT 40[MAKE "INC :INC+2 CIRCLE :INC]
END
```

and we produce the effect of Figure 6.12, which is a series of circles all touching at the same point and slowly getting larger. Unless one

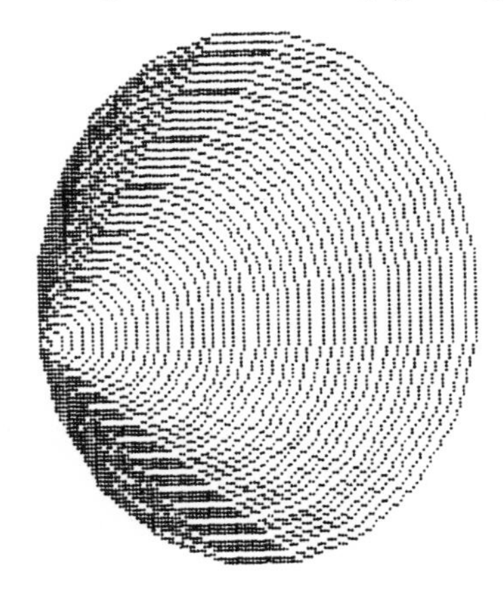

*Fig. 6.12.* Circles 1.

knew, it might be thought that this was some complex effect to portray the shading on a distant planet.

Looking carefully at the effect, and knowing what we do, we can discern how the straight edges to the circle become more noticeable. The most clearly visible are those sides which are either horizontal or vertical. A careful person might be able to count five straight lines per quarter circle.

I noted earlier that my graphical resolution was better than most (my pixels are smaller, and there are more of them). Figure 6.13 shows exactly the same routine (to the same scale) in a lower resolution graphical mode.

Notice how in the second example the lines to the circles are that much thicker, and how the total effect looks so much coarser, and fairly different to the finer version. The second example is closer to the normal resolution for most LOGOs.

What we have encountered are called 'interference patterns' or sometimes 'moiré' or 'shot silk' patterns. If one has a piece of very fine silk, with its lines of thread going horizontally and vertically,

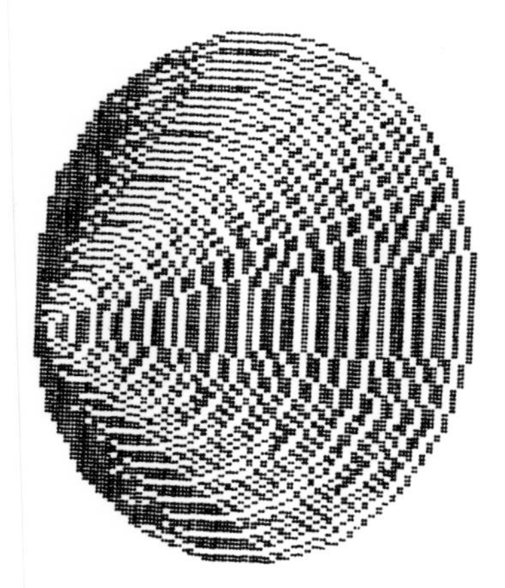

*Fig. 6.13.* Circles 2.

and then one draws lines across the fabric, close together, a shot silk effect is produced. The shot silk effect is also called a moiré effect, or a moiré pattern.

By drawing lines of colour on the silk, we are replicating the effect of drawing lines on the computer screen (or should it be vice versa?). The line on the silk is a series of dabs which can only catch on the horizontal and vertical threads. As the colour does not spread, we get a similar effect with pixels. This is particularly noticeable in Figure 6.13.

## Graphing a function

We can modify CIRCLE to draw another shape.

```
TO CIRCLE.TRIG :INC
  LOCAL "J
  MAKE "J 0
  REPEAT 20 [MAKE "J :J 18 FORWARD ABS SIN :J
    RIGHT 18]
END
```

In the above program, CIRCLE.TRIG varies the length of side of the 20-sided polygon according to the absolute size of the sine of the angle turned through by the turtle so far in its total trip. I use the absolute value because otherwise the curve will not return to base – but more of that later.

The sequence:

```
CIRCLE.TRIG 100
RIGHT 180
CIRCLE.TRIG 100
```

results in Figure 6.14. The two curves are exactly the same, but one is turned through 180 degrees.

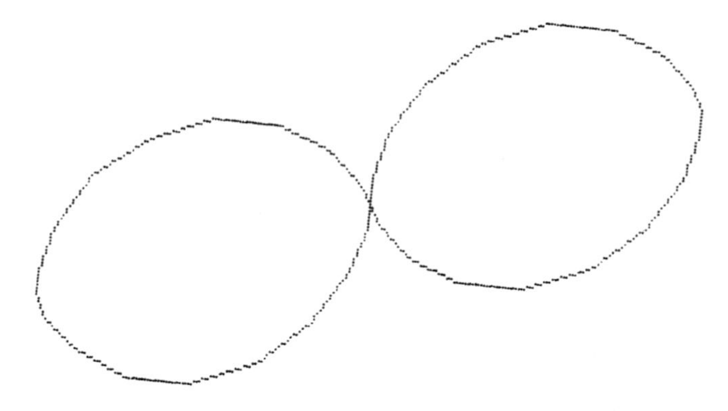

*Fig. 6.14.* SIN function.

The reason why I inserted the ABS (for 'absolute value') in the FORWARD parameter was because I did not get a closed curve. Instead, I produced a curve which looked just like a conventional picture of a bird – that is, two curved lines joined in the centre.

As a final fling, I substituted COS for SIN to produce Figure 6.15.

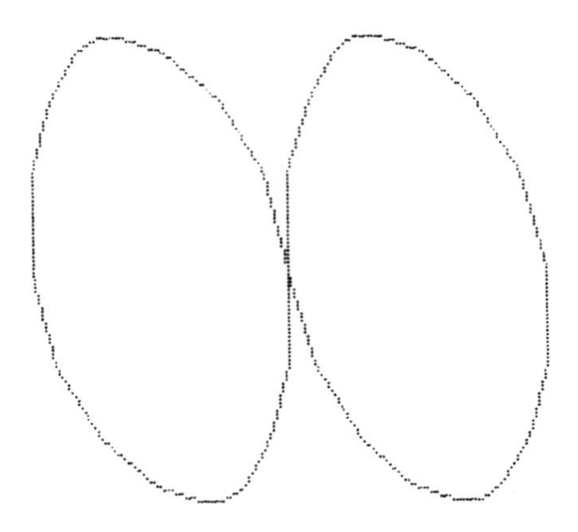

*Fig. 6.15.* COS function.

The two curves are very similar to the previous two, but with each separate figure rotated through 90 degrees. Funnily enough, COS

:ANGLE = SIN (9Ø – :ANGLE), so perhaps that is why? There is plenty here to keep fairly advanced learners busy.

Graphics is fun (and some of the examples in earlier chapters show that clearly, perhaps more clearly than this chapter). However, graphics can also be used very easily to present esoteric information in a manageable way.

# Chapter Seven
# Lists, Words, and Naming LOGO

Words are all we have.

Samuel Beckett

As I have noted on many occasions, LOGO takes many ideas from LISP. For at least one version (that from Edinburgh) the similarity to LISP is very close, and programs in LOGO and LISP have many common features.

LISP was developed to manipulate lists of items (called 'atoms') and has been very successful in artificial intelligence work. There is a strong argument that in education many of the problems with conventional programming methods, and ways of using computers, might be ameliorated by an intelligent application of ideas from artificial intelligence.

A recent book on this subject, *Learning and Teaching with Computers – Artificial Intelligence in Education* by Tim O'Shea and John Self (1983), claims that 'The designers of computer systems to be used in education should take account of the subject of artificial intelligence, and the users of such systems may expect them soon to provide facilities considerably more sophisticated than those available today'. Both authors have been associated with Edinburgh University in some way or other.

## Words again

We have already touched on the difference between names and values, so what is in a name? LOGO treats any sequence of printable characters (with some exceptions) as a legitimate word. A word is basically a chunk of characters which can all be used as a unit. Words need not be as they seem:

```
PRINT "A.WORD
>> A.WORD
PRINT "100
>> 100
PRINT 100
>> 100
PRINT "100/2
>> 100/2
PRINT 100/2
>>50
PRINT A.WORD
>> **THERE IS NO PROCEDURE CALLED A.WORD
```

so let us go through the sequence.

"A.WORD is treated by LOGO as a word (though RML would use 'A.WORD), as is "100. So, to ask it to print out "A.WORD is the same as asking it to print out A. WORD. When it prints out "100 as 100, the system does not consider that the item it is printing out is the number 100; it is the string of characters 1,0, and 0.

To print out "100/2 is to ask the system to print out the string of five characters, the word "100/2. To leave out the preceding quote is to ask the system to evaluate the expression, to produce a result, and the result is 50.

The set of characters A.WORD, without the preceding quote, is also treated by LOGO as something to be evaluated. As it is not a number, LOGO thinks it must be a procedure, but as it is not (we accidentally missed the quote from the front), LOGO gives an error message.

In a sense, LOGO – like LISP before it – treats the sequence "A.WORD as a list of characters, so that is why so many of the list-manipulating procedures of LOGO can be used on words. A word is the basic list. In some LOGOs (e.g. Atari LOGO), where words and lists are treated as being in some way the same, the general word/list is called an object.

A word can also be evaluated, just as can a number or a procedure, and how it is evaluated depends on the context:

```
PRINT "100/2
>> 100/2
PRINT "100 / 2
>> 50
```

LOGO encounters PRINT, so it knows that it has to expect something to print. It next encounters "100, so it is ready to print

100 – the space after "100 signals the end of that word. Next in the sequence is / and so LOGO then expects to have to divide the number it already has, by the number to come.

There is no number, just the word "100, and so the LOGO translator sees if that word could be treated as if it were a number, and it can. The final item in the print list is 2, so that is divided into 100 to produce the result 50, which is then printed.

### Making names

We have met MAKE before, in the context of numbers. For example:

```
MAKE "VAR 3+4
PRINT :VAR
>> 7
```

Here the name is "VAR and the value contained in VAR (shown by :VAR) is 7. We can make more complex things.

Take the IF statement (either Apple LOGO or Atari LOGO, for example). There is no THEN or ELSE, and it takes the form

```
IF TRUTH.VALUE [ACTION.TRUE] [ACTION.FALSE]
```

So, to emulate

```
IF :N < 0 [STOP] [PRINT "POSITIVE]
```

we must first work out what is happening. If a value :N is less than 1 then stop, otherwise print out the word POSITIVE. Here goes:

```
MAKE "CONDITION [:N < 0]
MAKE "TRUE.RESULT [STOP]
MAKE "FALSE.RESULT [PRINT "POSITIVE]
```

and then

```
IF RUN :CONDITION :TRUE.RESULT :FALSE.RESULT
```

to perform the test. All the variables are lists, that is, sets of consecutive items delimited by [ and ].

The first list is composed of three items :N, <, and 0: and to activate this list as a condition, we have to treat it as if it were composed of instructions. This is the meaning of RUN – treat the following list as if it were program instructions.

The second and third lists are treated as lists by the IF, and so they do not need modifying in any way. Suppose we try

```
MAKE "OPUS1 [ [INTRODUCING LOGO] [BORIS
  ALLAN] [GRANADA PUBLISHING] ]
```

and then we investigate, for example,

```
PRINT FIRST :OPUS1
>> [INTRODUCING LOGO]
PRINT FIRST BUTFIRST :OPUS1
>> [BORIS ALLAN]
PRINT FIRST FIRST BUTFIRST :OPUS1
>> BORIS
PRINT FIRST FIRST FIRST BUTFIRST :OPUS1
>> B
```

to see how lists can be embedded in lists, how words are embedded in lists, and how letters (or 'characters') are embedded in words.

This is a simple example, but think how it could be extended:

```
MAKE "OPUS2 [ [ANNA KARENINA] [LEO TOLSTOY]
  [OXFORD UNIVERSITY PRESS] ]
MAKE "CATALOGUE [ :OPUS1 :OPUS2]
PRINT FIRST :CATALOGUE
>> [ [INTRODUCING LOGO] [BORIS ALLAN]
  [GRANADA PUBLISHING] ]
PRINT LAST LAST :CATALOGUE
>> [OXFORD UNIVERSITY PRESS]
```

and soon we could have the British Library at our finger tips.

## Lists

When we come to manipulate symbols, rather than numbers, lists are very useful ways of proceeding (this is why my main example, in Chapter 9, is mainly list processing, no turtle graphics, and few numbers).

If you think back to the search tree, perhaps you can see some congruences with list processing. In the analysis of lists, there are two ways of getting at parts of the list. We can find the first element (by use of FIRST) or all but the first element (i.e. BUTFIRST). Alternatively, we can extract the last element (i.e. LAST) or all but the last (i.e. BUTLAST).

Both these choices are binary, and to extract LEO from the "CATALOGUE, we choose the LAST element of "CATALOGUE (i.e. :OPUS2). We then find all BUTFIRST of "OPUS2 (i.e. [ [LEO

TOLSTOY] [OXFORD UNIVERSITY PRESS] ] ), so all we need is the FIRST of this remaining list (a list of two elements, the name of a person and his publisher).

```
PRINT FIRST BUTFIRST LAST :CATALOGUE
>> [LEO TOLSTOY]
```

We search through a tree, eliminating alternatives.

The whole topic of list processing is far more technical (in the sense of the ideas involved) and LOGO can be used for very complex purposes. It has been found that LOGO is eminently suitable for constructing adventure games, in which the adventure takes place in sets of highly interconnected scenes. The scenes are set up as lists of lists of environments.

Here is a dummy game:

```
TO ADVENTURE
  LOCAL "LOCATION "CARRIES
  PRINT
  PRINT [AMAZING MAZE]
  MAKE "LOCATION "START
  MAKE "CARRIES [ ]
  JOURNEY :LOCATION :CARRIES
END

TO JOURNEY :LOC :CARRY
  DESCRIBE :LOC
  MAKE "CARRY ACTION
  MAKE "LOC MOVEMENT
  JOURNEY :LOC :CARRY
END
```

Here, DESCRIBE is a procedure which describes the location. The location is itself a list and the words in the list actually give the description of that location. ACTION is a procedure which allows the adventurer to fight, pick up items or discard them, storing the new list of items in "CARRY.

The adventurer moves by the procedure MOVEMENT, which outputs the value of the new room to be stored in "LOC. The JOURNEY is continued by a recursive call to JOURNEY. I will not expand any more on this game but it can be seen how it would develop.

Lists will appear in the next chapter when we see how we control LOGO, though (as we have seen) the true control in LOGO comes from the way in which it is written.

## Linked lists

Lists can be used to examine how a computer works, and they can also be used to discover how to store information flexibly. Look at this list:

```
MAKE "X1 [ :CONTENT1 "X2 ]
```

The list X1 has two parts – the first element we will suppose contains the value of CONTENT1, and the second element contains the name X2. We find (assuming the value of CONTENT1 is [THIS IS X1]) that:

```
PRINT FIRST :X1
>> [THIS IS X1]
PRINT LAST :X1
>> X2
```

To obtain the value stored in X2 we use the LOGO word THING (or VALUE in RML LOGO), to produce

```
PRINT THING LAST :X1
>> [THIS IS X2] X3
```

and this is explained by the assignment

```
MAKE "X2 [ [THIS IS X2]"X3]
```

We now have what is termed *linked lists* (see Figure 7.1).

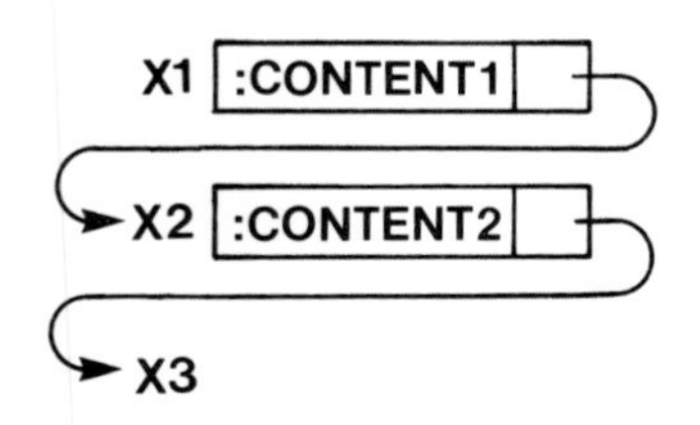


*Fig. 7.1.* A linked list.

Linked lists allow us to go through an ordered sequence of items, and also allow us easily to insert a new item in the sequence. Try a little example of landmarks and distances on a motorway.

Each item will be of the general form: first, the name of the landmark; second, the distance from the previous landmark; and, third, the name of the next landmark. The form is:

```
MAKE "LANDMARK [:NAME :DISTANCE "NEXT.
  LANDMARK]
```

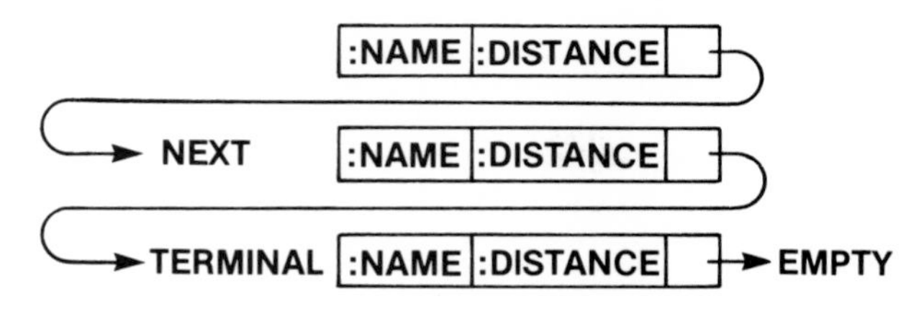


*Fig. 7.2.* Linked landmarks.

And, as motorways (thankfully) do not go on forever, we must reach a TERMINAL. The last landmark thus points to the TERMINAL (i.e. the final item is not the NEXT.LANDMARK, it is the TERMINAL) where we might define

MAKE "TERMINAL [[END OF MOTORWAY] 0 [ ]]

In any list of items we have to know where to stop. The idea behind this use of lists is shown in Figure 7.2.

The third element is called a 'pointer', it 'points' to the next item in a set of linked lists. We can access the third element by:

PRINT LAST :LANDMARK
>> NEXT.LANDMARK

To access the NAME given to the third element, we might then use THING, to get at the value of the third element,

PRINT FIRST THING LAST :LANDMARK
>> [WATFORD GAP SERVICES]

and to find the distance from the Watford Gap Services to the previous LANDMARK

PRINT FIRST BUTFIRST THING LAST :LANDMARK
>> [AN ETERNITY]

Note that the distance does not necessarily have to be numerical!

Suppose a new landmark is created (an almost permanent road works, for example). How could a new landmark be inserted? Let there be two landmarks X and Z (and after Z there is A):

MAKE "X [[FIRST OLD] 90 "Z]
MAKE "Z [[SECOND OLD] 11 "A]

X is the FIRST OLD landmark, which is 90 units away from the previous landmark, and Z is the next landmark. Z is the SECOND OLD landmark, it is 11 units away from X, and the next landmark on from Z is A (see Figure 7.3).

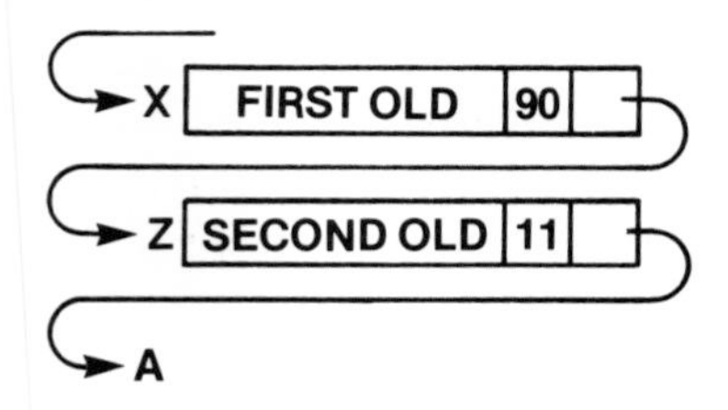


*Fig. 7.3.* Two landmarks.

A new landmark appears between X and Z – obviously it must be Y. Y is 9 units from X and 2 units from Z (11=9+2). There are rather more sophisticated ways of achieving the insertion of Y between X and Z, but here are the bare bones of the method:

```
MAKE "X LIST BUTLAST "X ["Y]
MAKE "Y [[THE INTERLOPER] 9 "Z]
MAKE "Z LIST FIRST "Z "2 LAST "Z
```

The first says MAKE the item named X a LIST composed of all BUT the LAST of the old list named X, plus the item "Y. The second is just a straight definition of what MAKEs Y. The final line says MAKE the item named Z a LIST which is the FIRST item of the old list Z, the word "2, and the last item of the old list Z.

What we have produced is a set of new definitions, equivalent to:

```
MAKE "X [ [FIRST OLD] 90 "Y]
MAKE "Y [ [THE INTERLOPER] 9 "Z]
MAKE "Z [ [SECOND OLD] 2 "A]
```

and you will appreciate that all this could be turned into a set of simple procedures. (See the diagrammatised form in Figure 7.4.) 'We could do all this with arrays', I hear some say.

For those who do not know, an *array* is an ordered sequence of information, where the content of each element of the array has to be of the same type. A distance cannot be a number or AN ETERNITY depending on how you feel, rather it has to be either a number or a description. Before we use an array we have to say how many

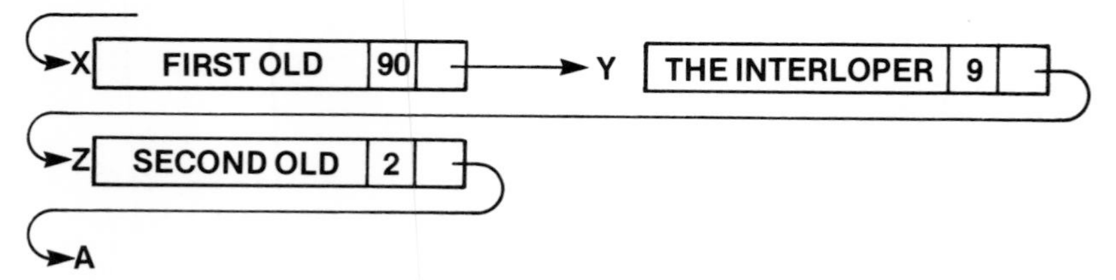


*Fig. 7.4.* Three landmarks.

elements there are to be at maximum – adding many new landmarks will mean we will run out of room in our arrays.

Linked lists are far more flexible than arrays – the adding of a new landmark with an array is also far more tedious.

### The program as a list

A list is a set of ordered items, and a program is a set of ordered items. A routine or procedure is also a set of ordered items. As we have noted many times, the idea of sequence in LOGO is very important. Earlier we cursorily examined the LOGO command RUN. RUN is a very useful command, because it takes a list (a set of ordered items) and treats the list as if it were a piece of program (which is a set of ordered items).

Some LOGO systems treat even the definition of a procedure as a list. For example, take the procedure SQUARE,

```
TO SQUARE :SIDE
  REPEAT 4 [FD :SIDE RT 90]
END
```

which in a sense is almost like saying

```
MAKE "SQUARE [REPEAT 4 [FD :SIDE RT
  90]]
```

To write SQUARE 100 is, therefore, equivalent to

```
MAKE "SIDE 100 RUN :SQUARE
```

with the added proviso that the value we MAKE for SIDE in the last line is only a temporary value (SIDE does not exist outside the SQUARE procedure).

To take this analysis slightly further, suppose we now produce a parameter-less procedure (because it makes life simpler),

```
TO NEW.SQUARE
  REPEAT 4 [ FD 100 RT 90]
END
```

to be followed by

```
TO TWO. SQUARE
  SQUARE
  RT 180
  SQUARE
END
```

Thus we have produced two squares diagonally opposite each other. In the MAKE form,

```
MAKE "NEW.SQUARE [REPEAT 4 [ FD 100 RT 90]]
MAKE "TWO.SQUARE [SQUARE RT 180 SQUARE]
```

where the last is equivalent to

```
MAKE "TWO.SQUARE [ [REPEAT 4[FD 100 RT90] ] RT 180
    [REPEAT 4 [FD 100 RT 90] ] ]
```

It is clear to see how program structure, lists and list-processing, cohere in the case of LOGO. It is also clear to see that the RUN command is not an add-on extra to the language, but is an integral part. Lists are tremendously important in LOGO!

## Chapter Eight

# Controlling LOGO

If he knew where he was going, it is not apparent from this distance. He fell down a great deal during this period, because of a trick he had of walking into himself.

*The Thurber Carnival* by James Thurber, on himself as a child

Seymour Papert tells the story of a girl who had written a game. The girl wanted to have a facility to run the game again, if the person playing so wished. After thinking about it for a while, and asking advice from others, she wrote

```
IF RL = [YES] [PLAY]
IF RL = [NO] [STOP]
```

where RL is the short form of READLIST, a procedure which reads in a list from the keyboad (terminated by a carriage return). If the input word is YES then the game should be played again (to start playing, one types PLAY). If the input word is NO then the procedure should be stopped.

What the girl had not realised was that the READLIST in the first line was different to the READLIST in the second line. The program would have enquired DO YOU WISH TO CONTINUE?, and you would have typed in NO. The first line would have checked whether YES had been typed in. It had not, so control passed to the next line.

The second line, however, expected another input. The user had to type in NO *again*, before the STOP was activated. Thus, to stop the game the user had to type in NO twice, but to play again the user only had to type in YES once. The obvious solution is

```
IF RL=[YES] [PLAY] [STOP]
```

but the girl and her friends had not yet met the 'else' list on an IF.

The moral of the story is that one has to keep in one's mind the importance of sequencing (here, for example, the first RL is not the same as the second RL). The girl, however, met herself coming back and said 'This computer won't take no for an answer'.

## Sequencing

The whole idea that the order in which things are performed is important is itself very important. As we found earlier, LOGO, by its very nature, tries to help children learn this important idea. If a child has to control multiple turtles, or multiple sprites, he has to get the sequence of events very clear – otherwise chaos will follow.

Multiple anything naturally leads on to the notion of lists, an assemblage of similar items, and in Atari LOGO there is a command EACH which takes a list as a parameter. The list is RUN for each active turtle, in the order of the turtle number. As different turtles can be different colours, EACH can produce the same effect at different positions in different colours, according to a fixed sequence given by the turtle number.

In Tandy Color LOGO there may be 255 turtles available for use and when only a few are active it seems as if they are all working simultaneously. At present, very few computers can perform *truly* simultaneous operations, and in the case of TCL there is an order to the operation of turtles. This becomes apparent if a large number of turtles are on the screen.

To produce new turtles, one HATCHes them. Here is the tree procedure implemented with HATCHing:

```
TO TCL.TREE :S :O
  IF ME = 0 (CLEAR SETY 0)
  IF :O = 0 (STOP)
  FORWARD :S
  LEFT 45
  HATCH 1
  TREE (:S/2) (:O–1)
  RIGHT 90
  HATCH 2
  TREE (:S/2) (:O–1)
  VANISH
END
```

Effectively, what happens is that each branch is given its own turtle (1 or 2, but that only holds within that procedure). The line with the

IF means that if ME (the current turtle) is number 0 (the master turtle) then clear the screen and go to Y=0, which for TCL is at the bottom of the screen. Though the earlier procedure for a tree is possibly easier to write for a person not used to TCL (especially if we forget about PENUP and PENDOWN), TCL.TREE has a certain extra educational value.

As TCL also enables turtles to communicate with each other, it can be very useful in that respect (though most of the newer sprite-using LOGOs have the capacity for inter-sprite communication). The main draw-back to TCL is the lack of list-processing.

## Control commands

The essential LOGO control commands are IF and REPEAT. REPEAT, however, is not a true control command because it is very inflexible.

The IF command is usually of the form IF THEN ELSE, where both the THEN and the ELSE may not actually appear, as in many MIT LOGOs. Apple LOGO has the extra (though equivalent) sequence TEST IFTRUE IFFALSE which has the advantage of being rather more explicit. There is, theoretically, no need for any other control command – but practically there are many reasons why others should be present. One good reason is ease of use.

Take the case of REPEAT. Suppose that we would like to repeat a sequence called "SEQUENCE, :COUNT number of times. We can either write

```
REPEAT :COUNT :SEQUENCE
```

or define a procedure RPT

```
TO RPT :COUNT :SEQUENCE
  IF :COUNT = 0 [STOP]
  RUN :SEQUENCE
  RPT :COUNT-1 :SEQUENCE
END
```

which has exactly the same effect as REPEAT. Actually, it might be worth altering the IF line to

```
IF :COUNT < 1 [STOP]
```

so that if a negative number were entered the procedure would not continue for ever. Note that all we need is IF and a recursive call.

In LOGO there is no GOTO command because it is not clear how GOTO might be used in LOGO programs (for a start there are no identifiers of lines, so GOTO where?). In some languages, the use of GOTO is frowned on, but it is not frowned on in LOGO – you just are not able to use it, because it isn't there.

The main way programs are controlled in LOGO is via the structure of the language itself, by taking a holistic approach with the emphasis on how the whole can be resolved into relevant sub-wholes. As LOGO is a list-processing language, it can act upon lists as if they were program text. Thus, any control structure one might want for the sake of convenience – and usually it is for the sake of convenience – can be constructed.

Some LOGOs have a few of these convenient extra commands, but we will try to concoct them, partly to see how they might work.

### Concocting control

We will implement a WHILE construct. While something is true, then do something; if it is not true at first then nothing happens. The definition

```
TO WHILE :CONDITION :ACTION
  IF NOT (RUN :CONDITION) [STOP]
  RUN :ACTION
  WHILE :CONDITION :ACTION
END
```

has great similarities to that for RPT, and a WHILE is a non-numerical version of REPEAT. In RPT we could evaluate the :COUNT directly, but in WHILE we had to RUN the :CONDITION.

If we wanted to set bounds on the movement of a turtle we might have a condition that the movements were to continue while the coordinates were within certain bounds. WHILE would be very useful at this point.

Another means of controlling a sequence of operations is to continue UNTIL a certain condition is met. The action is best explained by a definition:

```
TO UNTIL :CONDITION :ACTION
  RUN :ACTION
  IF (RUN :CONDITION) [STOP]
  UNTIL :CONDITION :ACTION
END
```

and the UNTIL is clearly an inverse WHILE. The IF and RUN lines are reversed, and the sense of the IF test is reversed.

We might use an UNTIL in some manner such as

```
UNTIL [XCOR > 75] [FORWARD 20 RIGHT 20]
```

This means 'until the X coordinate is greater than 75, make these moves'. An almost similar WHILE is

```
WHILE [XCOR < 75] [FORWARD 20 RIGHT 20]
```

This means 'make these moves while the X coordinate is less than 75'.

A final control beloved by some is the loop construct:

```
TO LOOP :COUNTER :START :END :ACTION
  IF :START > :END [STOP]
  MAKE :COUNTER :START
  RUN :ACTION
  LOOP :COUNTER (:START+1) :END :ACTION
END
```

This could also be written as

```
LOOP "I 1 20 [PRINT :I*:I]
```

where :I is the value of the loop counter, 1 the starting value, 20 the end value, and [PRINT :I*:I] the action to be initiated (printing out the squares of numbers from 1 to 20). This is the most complex of the procedures to understand.

The IF line is pretty easy to follow – it is the next line which might cause difficulty (though we discussed a similar state of affairs earlier). MAKE the *value* of COUNTER take the value START, that is, do not make the *name* "COUNTER take the value of START. The value of COUNTER is in fact I, and so the MAKE assigns the value of START to I.

However, as I have stressed all along, the important aspect is that of *recursion*, which combined with just one binary decision method (IF THEN ELSE) can be used to form all these items. Personally, I do not see much need for a looping procedure in LOGO.

I hope to have shown that only IF and recursion are needed to control the flow of a program. In what follows I will ignore the LOOP method of control. This is partly because it is only an unsophisticated version of the WHILE construct (it is so restrictive), and partly because it is not necessary.

The best way of controlling the progress of a program is to

construct it well, in a sensible and coherent manner (and by now you will have realised that a program is only another procedure). LOGO as a language leads to well-constructed programs by the way in which it is designed.

By accentuating the importance of procedures, and a procedural way of thinking, LOGO helps the user to begin to think in a coherent way about programming (and about thinking). To illustrate the benefits of the procedural mode of programming let us examine the above control mechanisms in more detail. In so doing we will show why we only need an IF THEN ELSE (however it is named) and recursion.

First of all, let us see what is the structure of the IF THEN ELSE combination.

## The basis of control : 1

The IF construction takes a condition, tests to see if it is true, and then if it is true proceeds with action 1, otherwise action 2 is instigated. But what is the basis of control implied in this schema?

The first to be investigated is the CONDITION. If the CONDITION is false (shown as FALSE? in Figure 8.1) the control jumps to ACTION2. When ACTION2 is complete, the program

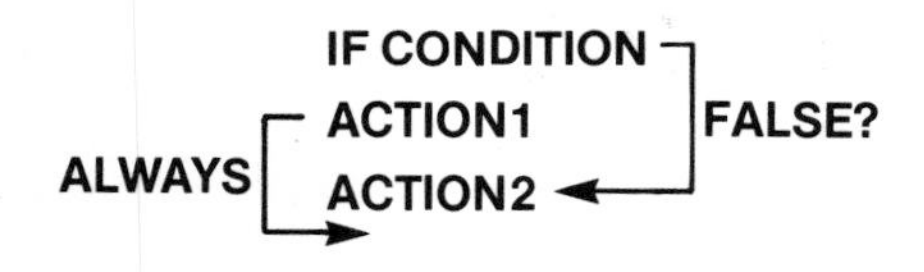


*Fig. 8.1.* IF control.

continues with the item immediately following ACTION2. As the normal way of progressing in LOGO is sequentially (i.e. one item after another) there is no need for any special operation following ACTION2; all progresses normally.

Suppose that the CONDITION is true. In this case, therefore, the next item in sequence (ACTION1) is activated, and no special operation is needed. If the CONDITION is FALSE? then the special operation activated is to jump to ACTION2, otherwise the default occurs (the next, ACTION1, is activated).

What happens, though, when the end of ACTION1 is reached? The next item (i.e. ACTION2) should not be activated, thus there is a need for a special operation to jump over ACTION2, and this 'jump' ALWAYS has to happen. In Figure 8.1 this operation is called ALWAYS to emphasise that it always occurs, i.e. there is no condition to be met.

In a more primitive language, this is shown clearly by the following:

```
          IF NOT.CONDITION THEN GOTO
            LABEL:FALSE?
          ACTION1
          GOTO LABEL:ALWAYS
FALSE?    ACTION2
ALWAYS    CONTINUE
```

Here the first line is the check on the falseness of the condition (that is why the item checked is shown as NOT.CONDITION). When the condition is not true, the control goes to the line indicated by the label FALSE? (In BASIC the label would be a line number, and all lines would be labelled – i.e numbered.)

The line which is simply ACTION1 is shorthand for possibly many lines (in BASIC almost certainly more than one line), and after those lines of program comes the line which is an unconditional jump to label ALWAYS. At this line the jump is ALWAYS to the label so named.

It is worth noting at this stage something extra to IF and recursion which allows LOGO to develop all these flexible control structures. LOGO allows the user to treat a list as a piece of program text and RUN it. ACTION1 (and ACTION2, below) are not fixed – they can be input as variable parameters. Unless a language has list-processing capabilities, this facility is rare. It is a very powerful facility.

When the jump has been to the line labelled FALSE?, the word ACTION2 possibly stands for many lines of program (as with ACTION1). When ACTION2 is complete, the program automatically (sequentially) progresses to line ALWAYS, so the same line is reached (ultimately) whether the condition is true or not.

In BASIC this sequence might be written as:

```
1000 IF NOT (CONDITION) THEN GOTO 1030
1010 GOSUB 2000
1020 GOTO 1040
1030 GOSUB 3000
1040 REM END OF SEQUENCE
```

but when we come to incorporate this little sequence in a program which already has line numbers from 1000 to 1040 (and possibly subroutines at lines 2000 and 3000) it becomes a trifle confusing. And it is only a little sequence! The use of GOTO can create much confusion in BASIC, unless the programmer is very expert.

The above point about variable actions becomes even more apparent here. How are we to change the content of subroutines 2000 and 3000, while the program is actually in progress? No BASIC I know will allow that to be done (unless you use machine code routines to PEEK and POKE, with much difficulty).

LOGO uses GOTOs, but it hides them in the IF statement, and thus makes them portable.

## The basis of control : 2

The other method of control which LOGO provides as part of the original specification is recursion. Recursion does not necessarily have to be used as it has been used already above to construct WHILE and UNTIL. The actual range of application of recursion is far wider than just control (as we have seen). Remember, therefore, that the use of recursion we will discuss in this section is very special, and not always true of recursion in general.

How does recursion work as a control mechanism? The sequence is very simple: a procedure is called (usually with parameters), and at the end of the procedure the procedure calls itself – possibly with changed values for the parameters. Note that the procedure calls itself at the end of the procedure: many recursive procedures do not wait until the end of the procedure to call themselves. See Figure 8.2.

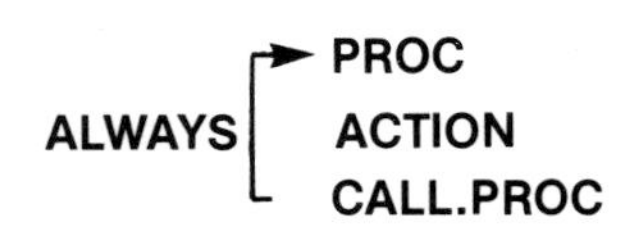


*Fig. 8.2.* Recursive control.

Let us analyse the flow of control again. The procedure is called, an ACTION occurs, and then after the action a recursive call is made to the procedure. In terms of the jumps made with IF, there is ALWAYS a jump made to the head of the same procedure. Any discretion (any FALSE?) must be part of the ACTION. Again we can simulate this unconditional recursion in a more primitive language.

First, let's try doing it in a non-line-number language:

```
ALWAYS   PROC                    (COMMENT A
                                  DUMMY LINE)
         ACTION
         GOTO LABEL:ALWAYS       (COMMENT
                                  A CALL.PROC)
```

Or, we could do it in a version of BASIC (two routines are possible)

```
1000 REM
1010 GOSUB 2000 : REM ACTION
1020 GOTO 1000
```

or

```
1000 REM
1010 GOSUB 2000 : REM ACTION
1020 GOSUB 1000
```

The latter of the two routines actually makes the equivalent of a recursive call in BASIC. The problem about renumbering, and merging routines still hold for the non-LOGO versions, though not for many other languages with similar capabilities to LOGO. Most languages which allow recursion still cannot cope with changeable actions, because they do not have facilities to RUN pieces of text as programs. Some BASICs have a VAL function which when applied to a string gives the value of the string, but VAL does not have the flexibility of RUN and a list.

A recursive control procedure is almost like writing, in LOGO,

```
REPEAT 32767 [ ACTION ]
```

where the 32767 is a big number, and probably the largest number possible for a REPEAT loop. This REPEAT loop effectively says 'Go on forever, almost'. The recursive procedure control will not go on forever because sooner or later the computer will run out of space in memory. Each time the procedure is called the LOGO translator has to keep tabs on which procedure has been called.

If the procedure has been called by itself 100 times, then there will be 100 tabs (in case at some time, for example, with the factorial, we go back up the procedures). Some LOGO systems, when they are nearly full, lose tabs on the early procedures (without telling the user). This is fine for the version of recursion we are using, but pretty drastic for other versions.

## WHILE revealed

The actual structure of the WHILE control command is shown in Figure 8.3, and the structure is very much in the abstract.

*Fig. 8.3.* WHILE structure.

WHILE comes to a CONDITION and, if false (i.e. FALSE?) a jump is made to the item following the ACTION. If the CONDITION is true then the program proceeds with the next item which is the ACTION. The ACTION is obviously variable, and is input to the WHILE procedure as a list parameter. When the ACTION is complete then an unconditional jump is made back to the CONDITION, which is again evaluated.

Earlier we saw how the WHILE control command could be implemented by use of IF and recursion. Figure 8.4 takes that implementation and shows how the control within the implementation of commands operates, in terms of IF and recursion. (Compare with Figures 8.1 and 8.2.)

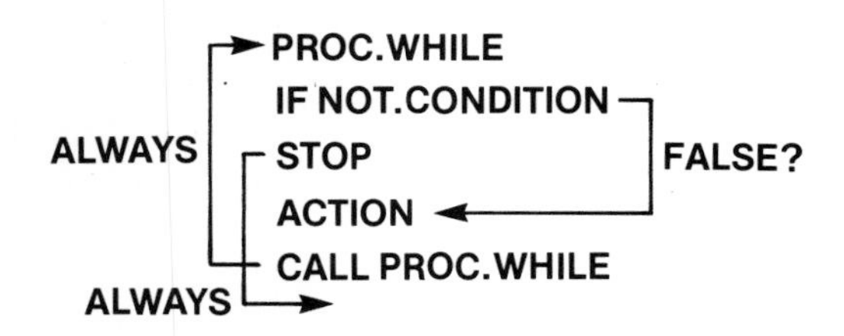


*Fig. 8.4.* WHILE control.

Examining Figure 8.4, the first line is the procedure line, with parameters, and the next line is the IF. IF the CONDITION is NOT true then control moves to the next item, which is STOP. STOP activates an unconditional jump out of the procedure (an ALWAYS).

If the NOT.CONDITION is untrue (i.e. FALSE?) then a jump is made to the ACTION. If it is not true that the condition is not true, then the condition must be true (work that one out). All this means that if the CONDITION is true then ACTION is activated.

The item following ACTION is a call to itself (possibly with modified parameters), and is an unconditional (ALWAYS) jump. What this means is that WHILE the (possibly changing) CONDITION is true, the ACTION will be taken, otherwise the looping will STOP.

It is worth trying to analyse RPT (see above) in the same way. Also, before reading the next section, try to see if you can display the UNTIL command. When you have tried the exercise, see if you agree with me.

## UNTIL revealed

The structure of the UNTIL – shown as Figure 8.5 – is the simplest of all.

*Fig. 8.5.* UNTIL structure.

The ACTION is commenced, and the next item is an UNTIL decision. If the result is false (FALSE?) then the ACTION is repeated.

Figure 8.6 shows how the UNTIL control command is implemented. There is a line which defines the PROC. UNTIL (with parameters), and an ACTION is taken without further ado.This means that the ACTION is bound to occur at least once, because the ACTION occurs before the test.

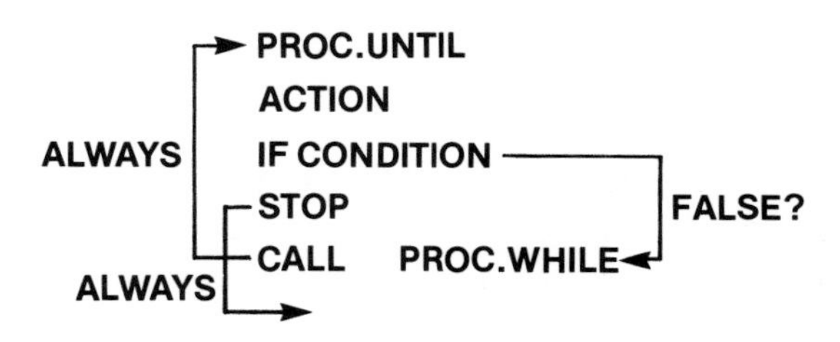


*Fig. 8.6.* UNTIL control.

The next item is the test. If the CONDITION is not true (i.e. FALSE?) then a jump is made to the item which is the recursive call. If the CONDITION is true then STOP is activated, which is an unconditional jump (ALWAYS) out of the procedure. At the recursive call, an unconditional jump (ALWAYS) is made to the start, possibly with modified parameters. Remember that the ACTION is a list parameter.

An interesting variant on the WHILE and UNTIL commands is the WHILE UNTIL. Try to plan the control structures for a system which operates WHILE something is true and UNTIL something different is true: e.g. WHILE it is Sunday and UNTIL I get tired, I will go to the gym. Answers of sorts are provided in the Appendix.

# Chapter Nine
# LOGO at Length

If the nineteenth century was the age of the editorial chair, ours is the age of the psychiatrist's couch.

*Understanding Media* by Marshall McLuhan

A classic program with artificial intelligence pretensions is *Eliza* or the *Doctor Program*. The concept was originally invented by Joseph Weizenbaum, also from MIT. He developed the program to try to emulate the practice of a non-reactive psychiatrist, that is, a person who never answered any of your questions but merely turned the answers back upon you.

Just after the program was first finished (written in LISP, I believe) he tried it out on his secretary, who got so carried away with her 'conversation' with the computer, that she asked Weizenbaum to leave the room. Her conversation was, she said, 'Private'.

This does not indicate that the program was intelligent, rather that humans have tremendous ability to imagine themselves to be part of unreal situations. There are those who are hooked on video games, there are those who weep at films like *Love Story*. In fact, humans have a tremendous imaginative power. LOGO tries to tap that imaginative power.

## Program outline of 'Eliza'

First of all we have to decide on how our psychiatrist is to respond to our questions and answers. How would a true psychiatrist respond?

A true psychiatrist would probably respond to what we said, but would also respond to what was unsaid, the implications and nuances. The psychiatrist would probably try to read the patient's body language. We cannot do most of that, all we can do is respond to some small part of what the user communicates, via the keyboard.

When something is typed in, therefore, we have to have the program examine the text to try to see if any sense can be made of it. The text will be stored as a list of separate words, and so we have to go through those words to find significant elements. Sometimes the program will not be able to find a word that can be recognised, so then we have to fall back on a different program strategy.

Somewhere we have to store keywords – words, that is, that we wish the program to recognise and to which we plan responses. If there is a 'YOU' in the input text we might wish to respond 'WE ARE TALKING ABOUT YOU, NOT ME' or similar. To each of our keywords we have to associate a response and, in a more complex version (which would take up even more space), possibly more than one response.

As well as those responses to keywords, there has to be a list of responses which are used randomly when there is no keyword to be found. The user/patient might enter 'XANADU' and there is no answer to that. We need a list of dummy responses, which do not mean anything, but use up time while the psychiatrist/program is stumped for a relevant response.

## The program

This program was written for the RML Link 480Z, using the Edinburgh version of LOGO. First a routine sets up the system, called ELIZA:

```
BUILD ELIZA
  NEW 'KEY 'RESPONSES 'DUMMIES
  SAY [WELCOME TO ELIZA – PLEASE WAIT]
  MAKE 'KEY [COMPUTER COMPUTERS PROGRAM
    OFF LIFE YOU I]
  MAKE 'RESPONSES [ARE YOU WORRIED ABOUT
    MACHINES?] [WE ARE INTELLIGENT!]
    [I LIKE LOGO] [NO]
    [LIFE – DO NOT TALK TO ME ABOUT LIFE]
    [WE ARE CONSIDERING YOU NOT ME]
    [DO YOU OFTEN TALK ABOUT YOURSELF?] ]
  MAKE 'DUMMIES [[REALLY, ARE YOU SURE?]
    [CAN YOU ELUCIDATE YOUR THOUGHTS?] [WHY
    DO YOU SAY THAT?] [YES, YES, I SEE]
```

```
    [WHY?] ]
  SAY [ ]
  SAY [WHAT IS YOUR PROBLEM?]
  SAY [ ]
    CONVERSATION
END
```

ELIZA has three new local variables, each of which is a list. The RML command SAY is like many other LOGOs' PRINT, in that it prints without enclosing the response within brackets (which is what it does with PRINT).

The list KEY (note the single quote preceding) is made to hold a series of elements, each of which is a keyword. For this example I have only provided seven possible keywords, for economy, and so that the listing does not become too complicated. Note that KEY is a very simple list, whose elements are all simple objects – i.e. words.

The next list RESPONSES is rather more complex. RESPONSES is a list of lists, where, for example, an element of the list is [WE ARE CONSIDERING YOU NOT ME], not a word such as YOU. YOU, however, is an element of the list [WE ARE CONSIDERING YOU NOT ME]. The elements of KEY are related to the elements of RESPONSES in a simple one-to-one manner.

| KEY LIST | RESPONSES LIST |
|---|---|
| COMPUTER | [ARE YOU WORRIED ABOUT MACHINES?] |
| COMPUTERS | [WE ARE INTELLIGENT!] |
| PROGRAM | [I LIKE LOGO] |
| OFF | [NO] |
| LIFE | [LIFE – DO NOT TALK TO ME ABOUT LIFE] |
| YOU | [WE ARE CONSIDERING YOU NOT ME] |
| I | [DO YOU OFTEN TALK ABOUT YOURSELF?] |

The reasoning behind most of the responses to keywords is probably clear, and the reason why OFF is singled out for a response of [NO] is that rude comments often end with OFF.

DUMMIES, mentioned in ELIZA, is a short list of non-commital replies.

The next procedure, CONVERSATION, was in the last line of ELIZA, and does a slight bit more:

```
BUILD CONVERSATION
  NEW 'PLACE 'SEARCHPHRASE
  INPUT
  MAKE 'PLACE STEP :KEY :SEARCHPHRASE
```

```
  IF EQUALQ :PLACE 0 THEN NOTFOUND ELSE
    FOUND :PLACE
    CONVERSATION
END
```

PLACE and SEARCHPHRASE are local variables new to this activation of the procedure, and the line INPUT calls a procedure (given later) to read in a string. PLACE is made equal to the result of comparing the list of keywords with the input SEARCHPHRASE (the procedure is called STEP).

If the value of PLACE is zero then there was no match, and a procedure NOTFOUND is called, otherwise the procedure FOUND is activated. CONVERSATION is then called recursively, and the process repeats (without end; there is no facility to stop the program, other than breaking in).

The INPUT procedure is very simple:

```
BUILD INPUT
  MAKE 'SEARCHPHRASE ASK [ ]
END
```

It merely requests input (using the RML procedure ASK).

The procedure STEP is rather more complex:

```
BUILD STEP :ALIST :BLIST
  NEW 'PLACE
  IF EMPTYQ :BLIST THEN RESULT 0
  MAKE 'PLACE MEMBERQ FIRST :BLIST :ALIST 1
  IF EQUALQ :PLACE 0 THEN RESULT STEP :ALIST
    REST :BLIST ELSE RESULT :PLACE
END
```

STEP needs to be seen in conjunction with:

```
BUILD MEMBERQ :OBJECT :LIST :COUNTER
  IF EMPTYQ :LIST THEN RESULT 0
  IF EQUALQ :OBJECT FIRST :LIST THEN
    RESULT :COUNTER
  MAKE 'COUNTER ADD :COUNTER 1
  RESULT MEMBERQ :OBJECT REST :LIST :COUNTER
END
```

Take it slowly. If you go back to CONVERSATION, you will see that STEP is designed to find any match between the keywords and the input list of words. ALIST in STEP is the KEY words list, and BLIST is initially the SEARCHPHRASE.

A new variable is made (PLACE), and first of all there is a check to see if the BLIST is empty, i.e. whether it has no elements. It could have no elements, either because the user returned a null string (i.e. just pressed return) or because in later processing the SEARCHPHRASE had been exhausted. If the string is empty (EMPTYQ) then the procedure returns a result of 0.

'PLACE is then made equal to the position of a matching keyword in the list of keywords, if there is a match at that stage. This makes use of MEMBERQ.

When MEMBERQ is first called, the third parameter is unity, and so :COUNTER starts at 1. A check is made to see if the keyword list (:LIST) is empty. If so, 0 is returned. If the :OBJECT (a word from the original SEARCHPHRASE) is the same as the first element in the list of keywords then the value of COUNTER is returned. If not, the value of COUNTER is incremented by 1, and the result of MEMBERQ is another call to MEMBERQ for the REST of the keyword list (REST is the same as BUTFIRST). The recursive calls continue until the keywords are exhausted, and so back to STEP. If :PLACE is equal to 0 then the result of STEP is a recursive call to STEP for the REST of the input list of words, otherwise the result is the value of PLACE.

At this point it might be worth going back over the argument to try to firm it up. Essentially, what is happening is that STEP goes through the input list word by word (i.e. by FIRST :BLIST where :BLIST gets shorter and shorter). MEMBERQ takes that word from the input list, and compares it word by word with the list of keywords (i.e. FIRST :LIST). Try to keep that in mind.

We can now examine FOUND and NOTFOUND.

```
BUILD FOUND :POSITION
  SAY :RESPONSES # :POSITION
END

BUILD NOTFOUND
  SAY PICKANY :DUMMIES
END
```

In FOUND, we have one of the few examples (and I do not know why) of infix notation. The # says 'choose the following element number from the preceding list'. In NOTFOUND, PICKANY is a provided routine to pick any element at random.

## The writing

The above program was written in a fairly short time by a fairly non-expert person – me. Though I had used other LOGO facilities before, I had never seriously tried any list processing. Apart from MEMBERQ and STEP, which were slightly tedious, it took less time to write than it would in BASIC, for example. What is more important is that it is easy to change the program to incorporate new keywords, new responses, and new dummies, without having to renumber and similar tedious chores.

This program shows the real power of LOGO, far more than the graphics – though the graphics are far prettier.

## A relational database

A database is an ordered set of information, a basis of data. A relational database is one which searches for information which is in a certain relation to the input query. People often talk of 'querying' a database.

Again, we are talking of an ordered set of items which, in the case of a relational database, is a rather more complex ordering. LOGO is very good at teasing out complex relationships, and discerning orderings.

We will construct a very simple database but, even so, this database is far beyond the capabilities of most BASICs or Pascal in terms of complexity. It is possible to construct a relational database in these languages, but the interface is very difficult to construct.

We want to be able to query easily (or, another term, 'interrogate') the database. In LOGO we do not have to use any special feature, but in Pascal and BASICs we do have to write special routines to allow the user to ask questions of the database.

We need two main types of user routine: one to allow the user to enter data, and the other to interrogate the database. In LOGO these are merely two ordinary procedures – there is no need to create any special effects. Let the putting of information into the system be performed by the procedure INFO, and the asking for information by WHATIS.

The data which we will relate will be very simple, of the 'PEOPLE EAT CATS' or 'LOGO RULES LISP' variety. There is an 'object' (e.g. 'PEOPLE' or 'LOGO') which is in a certain defined relation (e.g. 'EAT' or 'RULES') to another object (e.g. 'CATS' or 'LISP').

The structure can be seen as the basis for many sentences – in a rather more complex form.

Suppose that we have put the following eight immensely interesting items of information into the database:

```
INFO    [BORIS LIKES LOGO]
INFO    [BORIS LIKES FORTH]
INFO    [RICHARD LIKES LOGO]
INFO    [RICHARD LIKES MONEY]
INFO    [RICHARD HAS BEARD]
INFO    [BORIS HAS EYES]
INFO    [BORIS EATS FOOD]
INFO    [LOGO IS STRUCTURED]
```

I want to find out everything I can about that marvellous chap BORIS, so I ask:

```
WHATIS[BORIS*R*O]
```

(The * prefix shows that this is a category to be examined.)

For this example, the answer is:

```
>> [BORIS LIKES LOGO]
>> [BORIS LIKES FORTH]
>> [BORIS HAS EYES]
>> [BORIS EATS FOOD]
```

and, to the query:

```
WHATIS [*A HAS BEARD]
```

we should find:

```
>> [RICHARD HAS BEARD]
```

## INFO and WHATIS

Let us start with INFO – written again in RML LOGO –

```
BUILD INFO :DATUM
  IF NOT EQUALQ COUNT :DATUM 3 THEN SAY
    [OOPS!]
    AND ESCAPE
  MAKE 'DATA PUTLAST :DATA :DATUM
END
```

This procedure mentions two lists. The first list is DATUM, and it should contain the three elements of a relationship – object, relation object. In the IF check, when there are not three elements in the list DATUM, the user is warned and an ESCAPE is made from the routine.

The second list is DATA, and it is a list of lists. The lists of which it is a list are relationships, and the MAKE line adds an extra element (DATUM) onto the list DATA. The list DATUM is PUTLAST of the elements of the list DATA. This routine tacks on valid lists to the end of the list of lists: it adds a datum to the database.

One part of the routine which might be puzzling is the portion NOT EQUALQ COUNT :DATUM 3, and to solve the sense of sequence we work from right to left (see Figure 9.1). We start with 3, and remember it: we come to the list DATUM and remember it: we then encounter COUNT, which is a procedure we apply to the last item we remembered, i.e. :DATUM.

The result of COUNT :DATUM (i.e. the number of elements in DATUM) is remembered. EQUALQ is a procedure which expects two parameters, the two items we still remember, and it compares the values of the two remembered items. The result of the comparison is a truth value (TRUE or FALSE), and the truth value is negated by NOT.

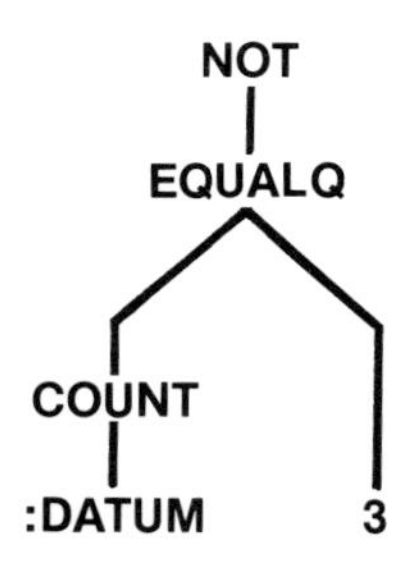


*Fig. 9.1.* Structure tree.

The upshot is that, if there are not three items in DATUM, the result of the portion after IF is true.

The other procedure we use to relate to the database is:

```
BUILD WHATIS :QUERY
  IF NOT EQUALQ COUNT :QUERY 3 THEN SAY
    [OOPS!]
    AND STOP
  INFOPRINT CHECK :QUERY :DATA
END
```

The IF line should be familiar, but the next line is less transparent. We do not know what is INFOPRINT or CHECK – we know :QUERY and can guess :DATA.

## CHECKS and PRINTS

INFOPRINT prints out information on relationships which fit with our QUERY, and CHECK is a routine which compares our QUERY to the database. Neither of these routines has been written yet. Let's start with INFOPRINT.

```
BUILD INFOPRINT :MATCHES
   IF NOT EMPTYQ :MATCHES
    THEN PRINT FIRST :MATCHES
    AND INFOPRINT BUTFIRST :MATCHES
END
```

The list of relevant relationships is to be contained in the list MATCHES. IF MATCHES is not empty THEN the FIRST element of the list (i.e. the first relationship) is PRINTed – to PRINT (rather than SAY) is to put square brackets around the output. Note the recursive use of INFOPRINT – this procedure emulates the equivalent of an UNTIL loop.

When we try to CHECK, we find:

```
BUILD CHECK :RELN :DBASE
  IF EMPTYQ :DBASE THEN RESULT[]
  IF SAME :RELN FIRST :DBASE THEN
    RESULT PUTFIRST FIRST :DBASE
    CHECK :RELN REST :DBASE
  RESULT CHECK :RELN REST :DBASE
END
```

First, note that there are three possible RESULTs to the procedure. The first RESULT is nothing (the empty list [ ]) if the DBASE list is empty.

The second possible RESULT is that there is something in common between the RELN and the DBASE lists (they are partly the SAME). In this case, the RESULT is to PUT the FIRST (matching) element onto the front of any other matching elements. The other matching elements are shown as being the result of the same CHECK on all but the first element of the DBASE list (i.e. the

REST). In this way each successive element of DBASE is examined to see if it has some items which are the SAME.

I will not attempt to go through the most complex procedure, that of SAME, but I will indicate how it might operate. We need to examine the first element of the database list, and compare it, item by item, with the query relationship.

We compare by looking at the first item of both. There are several options: the lists are both empty, or one is empty, so exit; or the item in the query list starts with a *, so move to the first item of the rest of the list; or the two items are different, so stop; or the two items are the same, so move to the first item of the rest of the list.

As an example, consider the part of SAME which examines the item for *

```
IF EQUALQ FIRST FIRST :RELN '* THEN
  RESULT SAME REST :RELN REST :DBASE.ITEM
```

This means that if the FIRST character of the FIRST item is the same as * ('* means the character or name, not any procedure or operation), then apply SAME to the REST of the RELN list and the REST of the DBASE.ITEM list.

LOGO allows us to put in a routine SAME as part of CHECK, without SAME having been written – this is very much part of the LOGO approach. The user starts with the problem and cuts it into little manageable bits. Each little bit then can possibly be further cut up, or treated as a whole. We can put aside difficult problems for later by saying 'Here we will have a routine to do this, and it will be called XXX' without actually writing XXX. If the program is run without XXX, then the program will not work, there will be an error, and the system will tell you something like 'I do not know how to XXX'.

To instate our database, we need to initialise the database list (i.e. DATA):

```
MAKE 'DATA [ ]
```

Then we can enter information by INFO, and retrieve it by WHATIS. Obviously such a system can be extended to cope with rather more complex tasks, but that is for more advanced users.

# Chapter Ten
# Why LOGO?

In this book I write about children but, in fact, most of the ideas expressed are relevant to how people learn at any age. I make specific references to children as a reflection of my personal conviction that it is the very youngest who stand to gain the most from change in the conditions of learning.

*Mindstorms* by Seymour Papert

LOGO began to be evolved round about 1967, by Bolt, Beranek and Newman, a research institute in Cambridge, Massachusetts, and the team which started LOGO included Wally Feurzeig, Danny Bibron, and Seymour Papert. Later, in the early 1970s, work began at Edinburgh University.

The early versions of LOGO focussed on words and sentences, but it was found that playing with words and symbols did not have the immediacy which had been hoped for. The language continued to evolve – as even now – and then Seymour Papert invented the notion of Turtle Graphics. The name 'turtle', the American for tortoise, was taken from Gray Walter's tortoise, an early attempt at an ambulatory robot (a moving hemisphere).

In 1972, at the University of Exeter, there was a conference on computers and education, at which Seymour Papert and some fellow workers (including Cynthia Solomon) brought along a version of LOGO to be tried out on what was then a large computer. Children from the neighbourhood participated in what Cynthia Solomon calls 'the first computer camp, ever'. The camp was very successful and encouraged others to try to use LOGO. It was at about this time that work in Edinburgh started.

Slowly, the language improved but it was still used on fairly large machines. Then, with the advent of the personal microcomputer, LOGO became available on microcomputers. The first microcomputer versions were written for the Apple II and the TI 99/4A machines (the first using real arithmetic and the second using integer arithmetic, though with sprites).

The language has now spread widely and versions are becoming available for most microcomputers. As there are now one million home computers in Britain, this means that education by computers, in the home, in a well thought out manner, is now a reality.

## How is LOGO learned?

Children should learn LOGO, so many of its advocates believe (as do I), by active engagement with the computer. The child is left to develop his or her own style of programming, (really, 'style of thinking') in a rich computing environment. The child should not be stifled by a rigid curriculum, with marks for progress when the child has reached a certain stage.

One teacher told me of her experiences with a very rudimentary version of LOGO – LOGO 2 for the BBC Microcomputer, a turtle graphics only implementation. The boys in her class were very keen at first, but as time went on their enthusiasm waned, particularly as the girls seemed to be getting on at a far faster pace. The boys wanted to get back to 'proper' arithmetic, with ticks and crosses in their book, and a feeling of safety, being on familiar ground. The boys felt they 'should' be better than the girls at playing with gadgets, but the girls discovered the aesthetic aspects to computing and the joy of discovery.

To have LOGO in a classroom does not remove all need for a teacher. As Papert himself makes clear, LOGO does not remove all need for guidance, rather it changes the form of guidance one has to give. It might be a straight answer to a question, a passing remark of the 'I bet you can't ...' type, or a session on the blackboard to examine why the sum of a geometrical series converges to a fixed value.

Another teacher (using Apple LOGO this time) found that, contrary to her expectations, children did not work successfully in mixed ability groupings (she had them working in groups of about four children). She also found that children worked better, and progressed further, in groups rather than alone. She found, in fact, that the streaming of children by ability worked, but she had to stream by computer ability, which did not seem to be too highly related to other abilities.

## What are the consequences?

The consequences for education are tremendous. Just as a child is deeply immersed in a culture, and grows up in a society, so LOGO is learning by being immersed in a computer culture. The computer is the most flexible machine yet developed by Man, and does not sit easily with conformity.

The conformist way of using the computer in education has already been suggested by some politicians. The computer is to be used to cut the numbers of teachers, because 'packages' will be developed so that children need only sit in front of a television, and do their exercises. The computer will mark the exercise and, possibly in time – so they hope – set the questions.

If we wanted a nation of conventionalist, non-innovative citizens this is one way of achieving that wish. This may possibly be one of the reasons for introducing computers into schools: ultimately, it is hoped, they would come to replace some of the teaching staff.

When we have nine-year-old children with great access to computers, with computers being used for constructive, nay, even creative, purposes, the education system will not be in a position to accommodate these children later in their educational careers. Many teachers will be able to cope, but the system will have many problems, particularly if the emphasis is still on the passive use of computers in secondary education. If the system tries to force children into a non-reactive mode of computer use, given the experience many will have at their primary school and/or at home, the system will be flaunted.

Though many teachers try to act against it, the structure of school tends to promote a uniform approach. If we care for the future there needs to be an end to fruitless uniformity. This is where LOGO can be so helpful, in encouraging children to assert their own individual creativity in tackling problems.

## Turtle graphics

Turtle graphics is a brilliantly conceived idea. Turtle graphics are immediate, gripping, and thought-provoking, but they also have a fascinating richness at the higher levels in mathematics – in topology and relativistic mechanics, for example.

I have included only one chapter specifically concerned with graphics, but many of the illustrations of other points could also best be made by using pictures. People react well to visual stimuli, and those graphics produced by the differential geometry method, which is what turtle graphics really are, have greater applicability than most.

The graphics examples I have shown could all be produced by more traditional coordinate geometry methods which require such an increase in programming skill that most persons would remain debarred. Most could actually do it if they had the time, but conventional coordinate geometry fits well with advanced mathematics, and not with elementary arithmetic.

Conventional coordinate geometry is needed, even by those who implement LOGOs, so the teaching of such skills will still be performed, but at a different time in a different order. It is interesting to note that UCSD Pascal (a programming language for the educationally more able) makes extensive use of the turtle approach.

When we come to turtle graphics, it is the 'good news, bad news' situation. The good news is that turtle graphics are very successful, and work exceptionally well. The bad news is that many people never think that there is anything more to LOGO than turtle graphics.

The number of 'LOGO' implementations which are only implementations of turtle graphics (and some are very good) is an indication that the success of turtle graphics has led to a failure to appreciate there is more to LOGO. I hope I have redressed the balance.

Seymour Papert strongly asserts that any LOGO worthy of the name should incorporate list processing (and remember that is actually where LOGO started), but when you say that a LOGO should have list processing there is often a slightly patronising look which says 'Who are you trying to kid? What good is that for anything useful in schools? Or anywhere?'.

I have seen elementary adventure programs, much as the illustration I gave, written by primary school children. An adventure game is a 'microworld', a special little pretend world where the child or adult can act out many vicarious roles. There are now LOGO simulations of historical events, which allow the child to be an actor in the events: all built up using list processing.

That LOGO is used for teaching on artificial intelligence courses at Edinburgh University indicates that the power of LOGO (on the computer in your home) is tremendous. You are limited only by your computer's memory and your imagination.

## After LOGO

At LOGO conferences there is always the question 'What comes after LOGO?'. As somebody commented, 'I wonder if they have conferences about FORTRAN, and ask what comes after FORTRAN?'. LOGO is an end in itself; it is remarkably flexible and has many uses.

It is, however, generally speaking, a slow language to run. Turtles often crawl round the screen, they seldom sprint. As it has well developed list processing capabilities, LOGO is expensive in terms of computer memory. LOGO is still happiest with a computer of large memory. This is not likely to change because, as LOGOs continually develop to capitalise on more hardware features of computers, so there is a demand for increased capabilities of computers. LOGO will always, I feel, be near the front of the capacities of our machines, and there will never be one LOGO.

At the moment there are many excellent versions of LOGO, all slightly or not so slightly different, and as machines develop new characteristics so LOGOs will also develop. There can be no standard LOGO, because that contradicts the exploratory nature of the language.

There are certain things that LOGO will never do well. For example, it cannot control devices as easily and quickly as FORTH. It is not, therefore, a universal language, and it is not intended to be one. Universal languages, anyway, are for people with closed minds.

# Appendix

Here is one solution, in LOGO, to the WHILE UNTIL control structure question at the end of Chapter 8.

```
TO WHILE.UNTIL :CONDITION1 :ACTION
  :CONDITION2
  IF NOT (RUN :CONDITION1) THEN STOP
  RUN :ACTION
  IF (RUN :CONDITION2) THEN STOP
  WHILE.UNTIL :CONDITION1 :ACTION :CONDITION2
END
```

The control structures are shown in Figures A.1 and A.2.

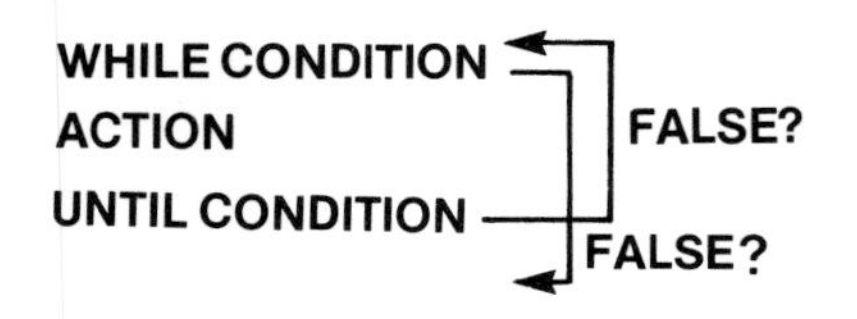


*Fig. A.1.* WHILE.UNTIL control.

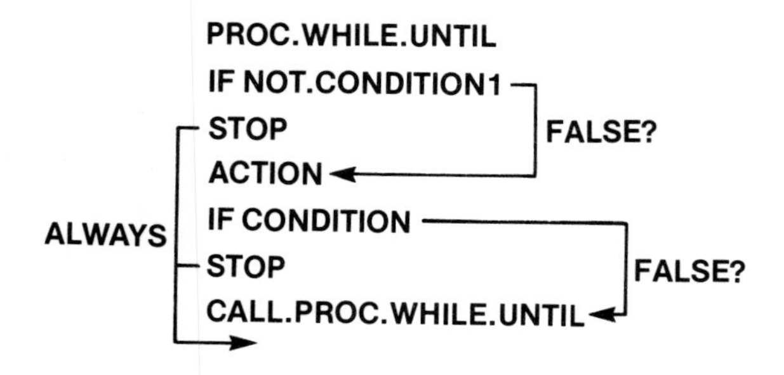


*Fig. A.2.* WHILE.UNTIL control.

# Glossary of LOGOs

It is never worth buying a computer just because it is the only one with a certain piece of software. If a piece of software is sufficiently popular, it will become available on other computers too, before long. If you are going to buy a new microcomputer, obviously, therefore, it is worth keeping an eye open for the languages which are potentially available. LOGO is available (or will be available shortly) for many computers.

LOGO comes in two main classes: proper LOGOs with turtle graphics and list processing; and varieties of turtle graphics. In the following list I will consider only proper LOGOs (though Tandy Color LOGO and Computer Concepts LOGO 2 are reasonable variants of turtle graphics). This list is not in any way complete, as no list could be complete given the speed at which LOGOs are appearing, and in some cases the information is based on that provided by the supplier.

## Apple II

Two varieties of LOGO are available, both of long standing, and both of a reasonable standard. There is Terrapin LOGO, and there is Apple LOGO, both of which are MIT versions. Apple LOGO is notable because it has the support of Harold Abelson (writer, with diSessa, of *Turtle Geometry*). Both versions provide list processing and real arithmetic, and come on disk.

## Atari

An MIT LOGO, with a good pedigree (Cynthia Solomon – Head of the Atari Research Laboratory – was in at the beginning of LOGO).

It is a list processing version, with real arithmetic, and with software sprites known as *demons*. It comes on disk or cartridge for any Atari machine.

### Commodore 64

A version of the well established Terrapin LOGO (see Apple II), with the addition of hardware sprites, comes as a cartridge (and possibly disk).

### IBM Personal Computer

Two versions of LOGO are available for the IBM PC. Waterloo LOGO (from the University of Waterloo, Ontario) is an MIT LOGO with additions (such as the unary minus), and comes on disk with its own operating sysem. Digital Research LOGO (i.e. DR LOGO) is an MIT LOGO, and it comes on disk to run under Digital Research's CP/M-86. Both versions incorporate list processing and real arithmetic.

### Research Machines 380Z/480Z

This is a strange, very idiosyncratic, version of LOGO developed by Edinburgh University. It has list processing and real arithmetic, and comes on disk. Personally, however, I cannot recommend this version.

### Sinclair Spectrum

This is an MIT LOGO with list processing and real arithmetic. It has been written by those responsible for Atari LOGO (and others) and comes on cassette.

### TI 99/4A

This is a new version of one of the oldest and most well-established LOGOs. List processing is not so well developed as with some other versions, and there is only integer arithmetic, but TI LOGO does have excellent graphics handling with hardware sprites. It might be the first LOGO to become available for more than one language (American, French, German, Italian, Spanish, and Dutch). It comes on cartridge, cassette, or disk.

# Index